SISTER EMMANUEL

Maryam of Bethlehem

The Little Arab

children
of
Medjugorje

Republished in 2020.
Book Design by Catholic Way Publishing.

Children of Medjugorje, Inc — Bosnia Herzegovina, 2011.
Original Title: Maryam de Bethléem, la petite arabe.

Translated from French by Anne Laboe.
Cover: Nancy Cleland, United States.

Pictures: Carmel of Bethlehem and Fire and Light Distribution: see website
www.childrenofmedjugorje.com

For foreign versions (French, Portuguese, Spanish, Polish, German, Dutch,
Croatian and Slovenian etc.) visit website: www.childrenofmedjugorje.com or
www.enfantsdemedjugorje.fr, Pray@childrenofmedjugorje.com

Ordering Information:
Orders by trade bookstores and wholesalers.
Please contact Ingram Content at www.ingramcontent.com

ISBN-13: 978-0-9980218-4-3

11 10 9 8 7 6 5 4 3 2

Available in E-Book.

www.childrenofmedjugorje.com

Contents

II. MARYAM, THE LITTLE PROPHET 55

I. The Little Arab

What a joy to know and to make known Maryam of Bethlehem! Commonly called the little Arab, Maryam, whose religious name was Sister Mary of Jesus Crucified, was beatified on November 13, 1983 by Pope John Paul II. Her life is a true epic. It is the story of the victory of light over darkness, of the Holy Spirit over the evil in the world. A magnificent light, one we need so badly today. Moreover, Maryam is young, imaginative, and original. She has traveled along totally unconventional paths, amazingly without ever having learned to read or write. She is an adventurer of the first order and, as well, a dear friend.

1. John Paul II takes her off the shelf

Maryam led an extraordinary life, a life full of wonders and lessons, but she remained in the shadows for over a century. It took beloved John Paul II to bring her out of obscurity for us! If now the Church reveals her to us, it is at the cost of a great struggle against the forces of darkness, a struggle against anonymity. It reminds us of Sister Faustina Kowalska, the first woman canonized in the third millennium, who was first cast aside, along with her writings, before Pope John Paul II revealed her to the entire world.

We must pay close attention to the life and the message of Maryam! After that long period in the shadows, what has now emerged with clarity has already nourished and enlightened many of those who are searching at all costs for the truth, especially the youth. We can consider it providential that Maryam remained unknown for so long, because her message resonates all the more today.

I speak of victory, because Maryam, during the course of her life, was tormented by terrible struggles. She received wonderful graces from Heaven to sustain her in her battles. Often, she had to confront Satan in person, and spiritual combat is one of the most enlightening parts of her teachings.

2. To begin with, a little anecdote

During my stay in Israel, I discovered the existence of this little Sister, and I was struck immediately — indeed concerned — by the intensity of the spiritual combat connected with her. A priest from Betharam, Father Jeangrand (+), found himself, like me, in Nazareth in 1977. At the time, he was chaplain of the Carmelite convent in Nazareth, and he had a very deep knowledge of the life of Maryam, whom he cherished in a very touching way. Hearing Father Jeangrand's stories about Maryam was like receiving an injection right from Heaven! My heart leaped for joy. He gave me a wonderful book about her, written by Maryam's actual spiritual director, Father Estrate. Because the book (in French) was difficult to find, he said to me: "Sister Emmanuel, take very good care of this book. Treat it like the apple of your eye!" So, I promised him to take particular care of it. Then, after leaving the priest, I took my car to go home, stopped at the corner grocery store to buy some bread for my community, got back in the car, and... the book had disappeared!

Back at the house, I picked up a brother, and when we returned to the scene, we found the book in a ditch, completely torn apart into a thousand pieces! It seemed as though a fit of anger had wanted to destroy this book. We saw that a car had run over it, reducing it to pitiful shreds, rendering it useless. At that moment, I realized the fury that the kingdom of darkness had against little Maryam, and it gave me great sympathy for her. When I went to confess my "crime" to Father Jeangrand, explaining to him that the book was completely destroyed, he said to me: "Yes, it's a shame! But that just proves that Maryam loves you very much, Sister Emmanuel! But that also proves that the Enemy does not love you!" I thought, "Thank God"! Of course, I was able to borrow another copy of the book. That confirmed for me the importance of digging into the message of our little Arab and of listening to what she had to say.

3. Daughter of Galilee

Maryam's story began in a very special way: her parents, half
Lebanese, half Syrian, were very poor. They settled in a tiny
village in Galilee, half an hour from Nazareth, the village of
Ibillin. Her father, Mr. Bouardy, made powder for dynamite.
Coincidentally, his own name meant "he who makes powder." The poverty of the family was only material, because the
Bouardy gave evidence of a solid, Christian faith. They
participated faithfully in the life of their parish, which was of
the Greek Orthodox rite.

The Bouardy had twelve sons in a row, but it happened
that these sons died one after another, either at birth or at an
early age. Imagine these parents who dreamed of starting a
large, staunchly Christian family and who saw their children
die one after the other! This trial was extremely cruel
for them.

After the twelfth death, they continued to encourage each
other and decided to take action: "Let's make a pilgrimage to
Bethlehem! Let's go there and ask the Blessed Mother for a
little girl. We'll make our way there by foot and implore her,
right there where she brought forth into the world the Son
of God."

So, they left for Bethlehem! Praying with faith and fervor,
they promised to offer to the Lord a weight of wax corre-
sponding to the weight of the child when she is three years
old. A little time later, little Maryam was conceived. She

seems to have been born without difficulty on January 5, 1846, just in the middle of the 19th century.

4. The power of intercession

Speaking of parents, let me point out the great benefit that there is for couples to intercede on behalf of their unborn children before the Lord. Before even being conceived in his mother's womb, every human being already exists in God's thought, in his heart as the Creator! "Before I formed you in the womb I knew you; and before you were born, I consecrated you," said the Lord to the prophet Jeremiah (Jr 1: 5). Through their prayers, couples attract great blessings upon their children to come.

Little Maryam is a beautiful example of that, because, from the moment of her conception, this child was consecrated to the Virgin Mary. Today, it is very rare to find parents who consecrate their children in advance to the Lord! So, when He finally finds such couples, I imagine that the Lord is so happy that He covers them with blessings! The Lord and His angels rush to this child asked for in prayer, to shower him with His predilections. Even when crises sometimes arise in the lives of these children, the Lord always remembers the prayers of his parents.

And this is the reason that, throughout the history of Christianity, we see the channelling of blessings into certain families. It is also very visible in the history of the Jewish people. "I have given you this, I have granted you that," says the Lord to certain figures in the Bible, "because of your fathers!" Parents have enormous influence over the holiness of their children. I think the holiness of little Maryam began with the prayer of her parents, from the moment of her conception. Her very life was obtained through the intercession of the Mother of God, and, all her life, little Maryam would enjoy a strong Marian protection.

5. The first heartbreak!

At the age of three, little Maryam found herself an orphan. There she was, already marked by suffering. She had a little brother, born around a year after her. His name was Paul, Boulos in Arabic. Maryam and Paul lived all their early years together. But, when their father and mother died within a few days of one another, they were separated. Now, in the Middle East, as in the Orient, where families are still numerous, orphans don't exist. Custom requires that, when a child loses his parents, he is immediately taken in by an uncle, aunt, cousin, or close relative. And so, there are no orphans.

Maryam's father died first. Sensing that his time had come, he took Maryam into his arms and prayed to St. Joseph: "St. Joseph, I, the father of this child, am going to depart, but I consecrate to you my child. Be her father, be her father!" Then he addressed himself to the Blessed Mother and said, "I consecrate my child to you. Be her mother, watch over her always!" And with these words, he died in peace.

It is very striking to see the importance of St. Joseph in the life of Maryam. As a responsible man, St. Joseph must have perked up his ears at the prayer of this father, so trusting. He remembered his supplication and took charge of Maryam. At many junctures in her life, St. Joseph came to visit her, to teach or protect her.

How beautiful it is to see the saints at work, and to see how they remember the dear ones that we have entrusted to them! They remember years and years after the prayer, even if we ourselves forget that prayer!

So, at the age of three, little Maryam was given over to one of her uncles who himself lived in the village of Ibillin. This uncle was much better off financially than the Bouardy parents. He certainly wasn't wealthy, but he lived comfortably all the same. Little Paul was given to another family in another village, and from the moment of this incredible and heartrending separation, the two children were never to see each other again!

6. The birds

Then, an event occurred which surely explains the elevation of Maryam's soul towards the Lord from her early childhood. One day, Maryam was playing by herself near her uncle's house. She loved to play outdoors, being very close to nature. She delighted in nature, in creation. She had the soul of a little St. Francis, always ready to be filled with wonder. She observed the trees, the animals, the sky, the earth. Later, when speaking of the things of God, her language was enriched with parables inspired by nature. Like those of Jesus!

She had observed, among other things, that birds never washed themselves. And so, in her childlike heart, she was overcome with compassion for these poor creatures that no one ever washed, and she decided to render them this service. She took a bird and began to wash it, to rub it, to dip it into the water, to apply soap, to rinse it... to be brief, the poor animal, as you can imagine, died of all this. Our Maryam found herself with this little dead creature in her hands: this gave her a terrible shock! The idea that she herself had brought on the death of this little animal shattered her.

7. The first call

Just at that moment, when she had sunk into this great childlike sadness, a voice rose in her heart, a very gentle voice but very loud at the same time, a voice she would remember all her life. This voice was saying to her: "You see, everything passes away! If you want to give me your heart, I will remain with you always."

For the first time, we see Maryam listening to God Himself, listening to Jesus speaking in her heart. We know that when "God says it, it is." Because of these words, perceived in the deepest part of her, Maryam developed a keen sense of which things pass away and which remain. "You see that everything passes away", the Lord had said to her. At that moment, Maryam became in a very real way detached from everything, even though she was still very young, only five or six years old. She was never able to recount this story very precisely, but it is thought that she was about five. Now that is an age when the Lord truly does great things in the souls of children. Maryam received this subtle perception early in life, that of distinguishing the things that pass away from those to which one shouldn't attach oneself, for fear of losing everything. And at that moment, she truly gave her heart to Jesus, without even knowing, of course, what she was committing herself to. But between that which passes away and that which does not pass away, Maryam knew to choose that which does not pass away. Her heart remained very marked by that childhood experience. She chose that day eternal things, those which cannot be taken from us.

Perhaps that explains why, from the earliest age, when she was barely six, Maryam began to fast on Saturdays in honor of the Blessed Mother. She began to do penances, to practice mortification of her body, and all without her parents' knowledge, secretly. She made a point of eating the things she liked the least and passing on other dishes. Why this understanding of fasting in the life of this child? It's because she wanted to dedicate herself to the gain of heavenly things and to demonstrate in that way her detachment from those things that pass away. That attitude of the heart only intensified throughout the course of her life.

8. When I was 5 years old...

I would like to emphasize here this act of giving her childlike heart to Jesus. Because among the contacts that I have been able to have with all kinds of people, one thing has struck me: very often, when someone converts after a life of sin, he says: "When I was young, when I was 5 years old, 8 years old, 12 years old, etc. One day I felt the urge to say to the Lord: 'I give you my heart! I give you my whole life. I want to live my whole life with you. I want to be with you!' And then, I forgot. Later I revolted against the Church, against the Lord. I rejected everything, I let everything go, I lived like a pagan."

But the Lord remembers that childhood prayer, and He is faithful! And one fine day, even though we have not thought about Him for a long, long time, up pops a providential event to turn us right side up, and the Lord comes back into our hearts.

I have the testimony of Olivier, who is now 23 years old. At the age of 11, he had an encounter with Jesus in his heart, and he said to the Lord: "Lord Jesus, I give you my life. I give myself to You!" Then, several months later, he forgot about it, and he even left the faith completely. After that, he traveled far and wide. He led a life of serious sin. He even dabbled in the occult. There, he grossly shamed himself with some hardly recommendable activities. And then, even in the midst of this evil, the Lord entered to recapture him! When Olivier returned to God, he remembered the prayer of his childhood:

"Lord Jesus, I give you my life!" He cried with joy at the memory! What he had forgotten, the Lord had remembered.

The Lord remembered his little Maryam, who, at five years of age, had given him her heart! He remained faithful to this sincere and innocent gift, and He would guide her with His hand. From that very moment, Jesus and Maryam became kindred spirits.

9. The story of the fish

From the most tender age, Maryam was truly called to be a prophet, to be a voice rising up in the Church. The story of the fish shows us that she had received very early in life the gift of reading into hearts and of sometimes seeing the invisible.

One night, she had a dream: she saw a man appearing at her uncle's house to offer a fish to his family.

But she saw that this fish had been poisoned and that this man wanted to kill the whole family. When she woke up, surprise! A man was actually at the door. She recognized him right away, thanks to the dream. It was really him, the man who was bringing a fish. The unknown visitor offered the fish to the family, a huge fish, and he said that it was a gift! Of course, the family was very happy and began to cook the fish for dinner. But Maryam pleaded with them, pleaded, "No! Don't eat that fish! It's poison! We're all going to die!" Well, then, everyone made fun of her: "What's this rubbish? Huh, childish nonsense!" She was not listened to and the fish was served at the table. So, Maryam begged to taste it first. Her goal was clear... everyone would see that she had died from the poison and then no one else would eat it. Even as a tiny child, she already had the inspiration to give up her own life to save others!

Faced with her insistence, the uncle and aunt finally said: "Hmmm, maybe we should pay attention!" And they decided not to eat the fish. They opened it and to the great surprise of everyone present, they found out that the fish had been poisoned by a viper. That day, everyone saw the evidence that Maryam was a special child. She had saved the whole family.

10. *The big snake*

This episode, taken among so many others, shows that Maryam was already living with the invisible, with those things of God that the eye does not normally see. She was already marked by a prophetic grace.

Here is another episode, one about a snake. One day, when she was still very young, Maryam was eating her baby food in a corner of the kitchen, all alone. It was a kind of custard. And then, up came a large snake, approaching her quietly. He worked his way right onto the table and was about to eat from Maryam's dish. But, at the sight of the snake, she didn't panic at all — she was undoubtedly unaware of the danger — and she even grabbed the head of the snake for fun, and, to allow him to eat faster, she dipped his head into her dish and began to eat with him. And the meal went on like that, like the most natural thing in the world! Then the servant came in... Horror! Taking in the scene, she let out a scream, and she chased away the snake, which was suddenly frightened. But Maryam remained in a state of complete calm!

From this episode, we can already guess how, in the future, Maryam would achieve her victories over the powers of darkness: it would be through her innocence and her purity! Satan cannot tolerate innocence. (That's why today he attacks so many babies, so many children!) But Maryam possessed the Number 1 weapon: by her innocence and humility, by the tranquility of her soul completely immersed in God, she would ensure that the Evil One had no power over her. Certainly, he would show himself, he would be in her hair from start to finish in order to attack her and try to make her fall. But he would not succeed, because Maryam would always keep her soul united to God, in innocence and purity.

11. Arranged marriage for Maryam

Maryam grew. She was about eight when her Uncle left the village of Ibillin and settled in Alexandria, taking Maryam and his family with him. He was very nice to her. He truly considered her a child of the family. But without her knowledge, Maryam was already engaged to a boy. This was 1858 and these arranged marriages organized by parents were a tradition in this family as in most Arab families, and it was completely normal in this era. The uncle and aunt had, therefore, arranged this plan of marriage for Maryam, and they announced to the little twelve-year-old that she was soon going to marry this boy, chosen for her years ago by her uncle. Maryam had no idea about any of this!

So, they dressed her in sumptuous clothing, offered her jewels, arranged her hair in an elegant way; in short, they made her into a most resplendent fiancée! But Maryam remembered that at the age of five she had promised her life to the Lord and had decided in her heart that she would never belong to anyone but Jesus. So, the wedding day arrived and Maryam began to panic. She pleaded and pleaded for the Blessed Mother to come to her aid and have this marriage plan put to an end. She went to speak to her uncle, but the uncle was strict. He absolutely would not bend in his decision. For him, it was imperative that he get his orphaned niece married. She would then be taken good care of, and that was the only future he could conceive for her. Such was the mentality of the times in that patriarchal society.

But the Mother of God was watching over the future spouse of her Son. So, during the night preceding the marriage, she whispered a little scheme to her protégée, a classic ruse that we can find also in the life of Saint Catherine of Siena. Maryam understood immediately and, first thing in the morning, she cut off her beautiful, long hair. Now it was unthinkable for a Middle Eastern man to marry a woman without hair! That just didn't happen. It would be a disgrace! The next morning, Maryam presented herself like that, without hair, in front of the family and the chosen fiancé.

She lifted her veil and then... Horror! There she was without hair, completely bald! Terrible! Scandalous! Maryam no longer had hair! As a consequence, she was deemed no longer marriageable. The scheme had worked well. Everyone was shocked at this act, and her uncle fell into a violent state of anger; he beat her until she bled, and Maryam carried the scars from his violent blows on her body. Then she was chased out of the family and found herself assigned as a slave to the slaves. In this family, it happened that several black servants were in the service of the uncle. These servants received the order to treat Maryam badly, to make her do the most difficult jobs, in the kitchen, in the garden, and in the fields, and, for several months, Maryam was submitted to this regime of persecutions and humiliations! God only knows what she had to endure at that time.

But, instead of rebelling or lamenting her fate, Maryam took up this new burden with a great deal of joy. She was already so deep in her intimacy with the Lord and with the inhabitants of Heaven. Although life was hard on the exterior, Maryam carried her heaven in her heart. She understood that her heart was a heaven, and, in the middle of the roughest work, she lived in joy. She gave witness to a real beatitude. That grace was very important for her. In effect, this rough work and this trial of rejection permitted her to strengthen her ties with God. Several months passed...

12. *Stay and have dinner with us!*

Maryam was twelve and she still remembered her brother
Paul, who lived near Nazareth. She learned that a certain
Muslim man had to go to Nazareth. So, she went to his
house to entrust him with a message to carry to her brother
Paul. That day, she was saying her good-byes to this Muslim
family, which lived very near to her own village, and, following the local tradition, they said to her: "Now, listen, stay and
have dinner with us. You can't leave already!" In the Middle
East, you know, you can't refuse an invitation. It's part of the
hospitality. And, besides, the day was beginning to wind
down. Maryam accepted the offer to have dinner with the
family. Since she had suffered some rather severe abuse,
people could see on her body evidence of beatings. So, during the course of the meal, this Muslim said to her: "Oh,
sure, the Christian religion, you see what a state it has put
you in. Those people are wicked. You ought to become a
Muslim, and then truly renounce your Christian faith." But
Maryam argued: "No, no, I'm holding onto my Christian
faith! I'm Catholic, and I honestly hope to die in my Catholic faith, which is the only true one."

And then, faced with the resistance of this little slip of a
girl, who was only a child, and of another religion besides,
the Muslim went into a rage: he kicked Maryam. The little
girl's chest was damaged, and she was thrown to the ground.
Then he took his scimitar and cut her throat! The wound was

fatal. So, his wife and he decided to get rid of the body quickly, and, under the cover of darkness, like villainous thieves, they took Maryam's body and threw it in a remote place, a sort of natural grotto. There, they abandoned her and returned to their home as if nothing had happened. It was the night of the 7th or 8th of September, 1858.

13. Your book is not yet finished!

What, then, was to become of little Maryam? We could say that she had suffered martyrdom: she had professed her Christian faith, and, because of her faith, she had shed her blood. It must be noted here that, when she was younger, in an outburst of love for the Lord, Maryam had asked for the grace to shed her blood for her faith. In fact, she was impatient to shed her blood for Jesus. The Lord had made her wait several years, but He had granted her prayer.

So, Maryam's body was abandoned in the darkness of this grotto, of this squalid little cave on the outskirts of Alexandria. Would the animals come to devour her? No, the story doesn't stop there! Something very mysterious was going to happen to this young adolescent, an incredible event! Years later, she would tell Father Estrate, her spiritual director, that she went up to Heaven, and that, there, she had a vision of God, a vision of the Blessed Trinity. She saw Jesus Christ in his humanity. She saw the throne of God. She saw the most Blessed Virgin Mary, who was standing near the throne of the Lord, in all the splendor of her glory. She saw the Angels of

God. She also saw the souls of the saints. She was immersed in a great, immense beatitude, in this happiness with no name that she could never really describe with her poor words, because, she said, it was indescribable.

Yet, in the midst of this beatitude — you could call it an ecstasy — someone approached her and said:

"Maryam, your book is not finished. You are going to return to Earth." Without knowing how, she woke up. She realized that she was in a grotto, and in this grotto, a woman came up to her. Her clothing was totally unrecognizable to Maryam, very much like the habit of a nun! It was a magnificent blue color! The lady simply stood there. She had an extraordinary gentleness about her, and her presence delighted the heart of Maryam. Then, the woman began to stitch up Maryam's neck, to care for her, to bandage her, to put ointments on her wound. The lady hardly spoke. Every day, she appeared next to Maryam and cared for her like a good nurse.

14. The most delicious soup ever

A profound, loving relationship was established then and there between Maryam and the mysterious nun; and then one day, Maryam began to feel her strength coming back. This lady had brought her very special food, something she had never seen! Maryam would say later: "It was a soup, but not a normal soup. It was a deliciously good soup." So she ate this soup with pleasure and asked for more. It was so good!

And then, as children do in front of delicious food, she said to the lady: "More!" At that moment, for the first time, the lady let her voice be heard and said: "Maryam, no, that's enough for the moment." She didn't want to give her any more of that soup. She seems to have used this request of Maryam to teach her a little lesson.

We know by what happened next that this lady, this mysterious nun, was none other than the Blessed Virgin Mary!

15. Always be content!

So, the Mother of God visited young Maryam in her grotto. Let us listen very carefully to what she told her: "Remember, Maryam, don't act like other people who think they never have enough! (This is still in regard to the story of the soup). Say always: 'That's enough!' Always be content, in spite of what you may have to suffer." Then the Virgin revealed to her that she would have to suffer a great deal in her life, and she insisted: "Always be content! The Lord, who is good, will send you all you need." She explained to her, also, that in her life, she must welcome everything as coming from the hand of God and that she must give thanks for every detail of her life.

For Maryam, that remained a luminous, decisive teaching! This "always be content" would form the foundation of her personal happiness and the framework of her consecrated life. Some years later, another Carmelite, Sister Therese of the Child Jesus, would explain the same thing in her own words:

"True happiness on Earth consists in always finding delicious the share that Jesus gives us."

Do you remember Psalm 23, which says: "The Lord is my shepherd, there is nothing I shall want"? For Maryam, those words were golden. She would take them literally. "There is nothing I shall want." Everything that happened to her throughout the course of her life, she would accept, from that day on, as coming from God. This attitude of the heart, that she chose to pursue radically, would make her the happiest of women. She knew from that time forward, that everything came from the hand of God. Whatever event presented itself, she didn't worry. On the contrary, she kissed the hand of God, even before noticing what was happening to her. Everything worked to the good in her eyes, so that she might take giant steps in faith and trust. In this way, she would seize the great happiness God offered in every situation, even the ones that seemed to be the worst. She made then, the right choice. If only each of us would make that same choice for our own great happiness!

That reminds me of these marvelous words of Marthe Robin, a French Mystic (1902 — 1981): "I see so clearly how much His adorable will is realized in everything, even in what is not wanted by Him, that I can only contemplate and adore in silence."

What does that mean? Well, God loves us so much that, when something bad happens which is not His will (for example, the consequence of a sin), He is powerful enough to bring good out of evil itself. In His almighty providence He can draw good from the consequences of an evil, even something moral, committed by his creatures. He uses it for our greater good. Another example: When Peter denied Jesus, that sin was certainly not part of God's will; but the Father used it; He turned the event around in favor of Peter, who, on that day, touched his profound misery, and was able to grow in humility and open himself to new dimensions of love.

-

16. No way we play into the Devil's game!

Maryam was not stopped by any obstacle, especially not by her own ego. Now, more often than not, when we are tested, we complain, and it is the complaining that stops us. Something happens that upsets us, and we say: "Oh, too bad, too bad. If that had happened some other way, at least I could have done this or that! Oh, if only my husband were different! Oh, if only that thing hadn't happened! Oh, if that illness had not brought me down! Oh, if only that person had not stolen my inheritance!"

In this way, without even realizing it, we play the Devil's game, by way of our complaints and our sterile lamentations; we bring ourselves to a standstill on our path to the Lord. Because the Devil, in the end, is the greatest complainer par excellence, he's eternally frustrated! He excels in deciding that nothing is going well!

He is always ready to rebel! But Maryam adopted the opposite attitude. Our Lady herself had given her this very clear advice: "Always be content!" Thanks to that, the Lord would find His joy in His little Maryam, and He would accomplish in her all that He wished. As the Lord said about King David, "I have found in David, son of Jesse, a man after my own heart! He will do all that I will." (Acts 13: 22). In a way, God prophesied for David. He didn't say, "He has done all my will." He rather said, "He will do." It's in the future! God is sure of David because David is faithful. David listens to the Lord. David obeys.

One could say the same thing about Maryam: a child after the heart of God, because she will do all that He wills!

17. God knocks on several doors

In His desire to communicate his infinite love, God knocks on several doors, on many, many doors; He searches, He hopes... How many times is He turned away? He longs to find someone who will say to Him: "Lord, You can do whatever You want in my life. I am content with your choice in advance!" God searches for such souls. And He discovered Maryam! He saw that whatever happened in her life, Maryam would say Yes in advance. In advance she adheres to the plan that God had in mind for her. So, what did the Lord do? He took advantage of that to lead her very, very far! He was all too happy to find the way unobstructed. With her, He could go forward without impediments, He could do everything! God would do all that He wanted in the life of Maryam, and she would realize all the potential for sainthood prepared for her. Potential for sainthood prepared for her? The history of the Church gives us many examples of saints who had to make decisive choices for their lives.

One day, Jesus spoke to the heart of a young Austrian woman, Maria Sieler (1899-1952), with the goal of attracting her completely to Him for a very special mission in the Church. Maria didn't say no to Him, but she was a little afraid. At the age of 24, while she was still hesitating to abandon herself totally to, He who called her, she heard this voice in her heart when returning from Communion: "If you don't want to go beyond what you are, I will search for another soul. I have thousands of other souls at my disposal, to whom I can offer my graces." Maria Sieler understood that the opportunity for this unique mission would not come again. She responded radically to the call of Jesus and became a soul on fire in her magnificent vocation of motherhood and for holiness for priests.

As another example, I have a friend who was called by God for a very particular mission in America. Since she was the mother of a family, she was astonished at Jesus after having been chosen for a vocation which, in her eyes, would have better suited a religious. But Jesus answered her: "Yes, I proposed this mission to another soul, but she told me No. So, I chose you, because you had said Yes for other things." My friend made clear with a certain humor: "Don't be mistaken, I am plan B!"

Our Maryam immediately gave her unconditional Yes to Jesus, and she knew that in acting this way she had opted for the best in this world and in the next. No one would take that away from her! This Yes is the fundamental attitude of the soul for the simple, Christian life. It is even more so for the consecrated life.

So, we shouldn't be surprised to see, in the life of Maryam, events which went completely beyond her capacities as a young child who knew neither how to read nor write, nor had any education. Who knew nothing of anything and who was so fragile, so delicate, and of such a tender nature! God would accomplish through her all that He wanted, because He had in His hand's malleable dough. Maryam accepted not always understanding what the Lord would do for her. So, He would do marvelous things.

18. You will die in Bethlehem

When Maryam was finally cured, the "Very Good Lady" continued to teach her. She spoke to her even about her future and described plainly what awaited her: She understood that she would never see her family again. She would have the temptation many times to show herself to them, to reveal herself. But the Lady's instructions were more than clear that she would have to remain hidden! It must be said here that Maryam was extremely attached to her family.

Maryam's disappearance was the subject of a great deal of talk in the uncle's family. They feared that Maryam had been seduced by someone, or that she had been kidnapped. Now, such an occurrence is terribly shameful for an Arab family.

So, they did everything to try to find her, and their searches extended absolutely everywhere. Maryam became aware of it very quickly upon returning to the world: everyone was looking for her, and she had to hide herself.

The Lady also added the prophetic words that Maryam would become a religious nun, that she would first be a child of Saint Joseph, before becoming a daughter of St. Teresa of Avila. Then she would take the habit of the Carmelites, and die in Bethlehem.

19. The nun disappeared!

It happened that, in the grotto, Maryam found her strength again and was capable of walking. In Alexandria, the nun took Maryam to a church, and said to the young girl of 12, "Go make your confession!" So, Maryam entered the church and said to the nun: "Wait for me here. I'll come back after my confession."

Maryam went to make her confession, and after the confession, she came out of the church and looked around for the nun. She searched and searched..." No, it's not possible!" Anguish mounted in her and gripped her more and more cruelly. The nun had disappeared!

Once again, a sword pierced the heart of Maryam. She had a feeling that she would never see the nun again, and for her that was a terrible thing! She found herself alone again, alone, absolutely alone in the world. Her family? That was over. She couldn't make contact with them. The instructions were clear. The absence of this nun, who had become for her a real mother, was insupportable. That was the agony in her heart. She no longer had anyone on earth to lean on! At that particular moment, she was in danger of losing her footing, but she remembered the words that Jesus gave her. She remembered the pact that she had made with the Lord. She knew that everything that happened to her came from God, and that she would never lack anything. She regained her courage. Then, she went to find the priest who had heard her confession, and, under the seal of secrecy, she told him her story. And this priest agreed to help her.

20. *The servant everyone dreams of*

With the help of the priest, she was to put herself into the domestic service of several families as a simple servant. Let's just imagine little Maryam, who at this time was only twelve years old! What courage it must have taken to get through these trials! She would go into the homes of rich families and poor families, into the houses of kind people and into the houses of wicked people. She began by working in Alexandria, but very soon she felt obliged to leave the city. Her family was still searching for her, and she was afraid of being discovered.

Her pilgrim's journey led her to Jerusalem, Jaffa and Beirut…. and there she came to experience poverty in some Arab families. The hallmark of this period of her life, as a servant in families, was her unstinting charity towards the poor, towards the sick. She brought them very tangible help: not only through her hands and her resourcefulness, but also through her prayer. She even performed miracles!

She famously put herself in the service of a family in which every member was sick. She went as far as begging for their bread. Through her prayer, each one got up from his sickbed or even his deathbed. Everyone was cured!

Another time, we see her with a family whose child had fallen from a balcony. Seeing him not moving, the family feared the worst but Maryam prayed. She cradled the child in her arms and invoked the Blessed Mother and the child was miraculously revived with only a few bruises.

There was one constant with Maryam, and that was the profound, heartfelt affection she manifested towards those she met. She often said, "Love your brother more than yourself!" That is really what she practiced and what she gave witness to. All these families were able to testify at the end of her stay in their homes: Maryam loved them more than herself.

21. Fearing God more than man

Why would she move from one family to another? Why didn't she ever stay very long in the same family? Quite simply, because of her great humility! She would arrive in her extreme poverty; she had but a single change of clothing and no other. She was received truly like a poor waif, and people scorned her. They would give her the most degrading jobs, and then, little by little, thanks to her effectiveness, thanks to her charity, thanks to the healing balm which seemed to reside within her, the members of that family would become attached to her and begin to have some esteem for her. The moment she sensed that this esteem was beginning to take root in their minds, or that she was going to be idolized, Maryam would slip away and go to serve elsewhere. She had such fear of falling into the sin of pride. She hated compliments so much that she would run from them. For seven years, she went from family to family doing good, curing the sick, delivering words of wisdom.

She could be extremely forthright at times. Whenever she saw sinfulness anywhere, she would warn the person. She was not afraid to give warning against sin, even to very important people. One day, for example, a certain woman was wearing a beautiful dress, extremely elegant and costly, and she was supposed to leave for a ball. Maryam warned her that her soul was in grave danger, and that the Lord was extremely unhappy with her demeanor, which was an invitation to adultery. This woman belonged to the nobility, but Maryam was not afraid to admonish her clearly. In short, the Lord and His glory came first for Maryam, and the rest came later.

For seven years, from 12 to 19 years of age, Maryam was in the service of various families, exercising humility and charity. Then, as had been predicted by the nun who had cared for her in the grotto, she found herself in the south of France, in Marseille. There she entered into the service of a family, the Najard family. It was in France that Maryam would receive for the first-time extraordinary graces and mystical communications from God.

22. First raptures

During her stay with the Najard family, Maryam experienced an extended rapture, which lasted two hours. People believed at first that she was dead, but the rosiness of her cheeks puzzled them! She was not dead and would awaken in two hours. To tell the truth, we will never know what happened during those two hours.

But, sometime later, Maryam would experience a rapture which, this time, would last for four days. The doctors worked desperately, trying to revive her. They gave her medicines. All the doctors said: "We don't understand what is happening in her. We have never seen such a case before." Much later, Maryam would talk about what happened. During those four days, her soul was introduced mystically into divine and invisible realities. Let's not forget the third beatitude given by Jesus, so very applicable to Maryam: "Blessed are the pure of heart, for they shall see God." (Matt. 5: 8)

23. We are created for Heaven

Maryam had the purest of hearts and she already saw God in this world. She saw heavenly realities, those realities which are actually much more tangible than the ones we can see and touch by way of our senses. She saw divine things and bore witness to them. During this rapture, the Blessed Mother introduced her to Heaven; she showed her Purgatory and Hell as well!

What can we say about the testimony of Maryam? It seems, today, that those heavenly realities have become unfamiliar to us. In our era, and especially in the West, we suffer a sort of conspiracy of silence about these things. We don't dare talk about them, either out of fear of ridicule or out of ignorance, because they have been presented in such a distorted way, so much so that we prefer to keep silent and avoid thinking about them.

But Maryam, like a true prophet, came to remind us of these things for which we were born. In her clear voice, the voice of a child, the voice of a visionary of heavenly things, she reminds us that we are created for Heaven; we are made for this union of eternal love with the Lord. "Our souls yearn for the courts of our God," says the psalmist. Our souls yearn and languish. They reach out for the Lord, and He is waiting for us in that eternal happiness which He has prepared for us.

In addition, Maryam, in her visions, met the Lord in His eternity. She met also, near Him, the souls of the saints. She met the angels, those happy spirits who live close to the Lord. She saw the glory attached to each soul! A glory which is directly related to what that soul has suffered for the Lord, what it had to endure for the glory of God while it was still on earth. Because as long as we are on earth, we still have time to choose God and to give ourselves to Him, to collaborate in the works of God, to seek His glory.

Maryam had tasted this happiness from the beyond. Why her? Why this privilege? Why did she get a taste of this intense happiness, this perfect happiness, this unforgettable happiness which is Heaven? We might say to ourselves, "Why her and not us?" But it is clear: if she tasted this happiness, it is because the Lord chose her from all eternity, so that she would speak to the world about this happiness! Frankly, everyone doesn't have the grace to be introduced into these mysteries from outside this world. It is not given to everyone to experience the taste of that heavenly happiness here below. But she received the charge, she, little Maryam, to tell us about it. She also paid the price!

I am thinking about various apparitions of the Virgin Mary, such as those at Lourdes, at La Salette, Fatima, apparitions which are now marked with the Church's seal of approval. How many times has Our Lady reminded us in these places, with insistence, of the final end of mankind? How many times does she remind us that man is not made for things which pass away? Man is not made to attach himself to things which can be taken away from us from one minute to the next, from one hour to the next! Man must prepare, starting this minute, for his eternity. Each soul chooses its own eternity; it is the soul which chooses the essence of its own eternity, in perfect freedom. That is very significant. But these things, so important to all, are rarely ever preached about. May they be preached about again, because, without this perspective of eternity, where is man headed today? As Our Lady of Medjugorje says, "This world is without hope for those who do not know Jesus." We are made for the things of Heaven!

24. The most reassuring insurance

I think about the way all the different types of insurance in our Western world have developed. We spend hours looking for the most assuring insurances, we can insure our houses, our health (which is completely normal), our jewels, our trips; we can even go so far as to insure our dogs! We spend incredible energy busying ourselves with these things. Certainly, they have their places. But how can you insure your jewels or your house and neglect to think, even for one minute throughout the day, about eternal life, about this eternity which waits for each mortal in this world? It's absurd! It's complete blindness! Oh, folly of man, who falls asleep on a powder keg with his pockets full of wretched insurance contracts!

Maryam is there to remind us that the things which pass away will pass away, and that all our insurances will pass away as well! Even insurance companies can pass away at any moment! It only takes a change of government! It only takes a disease, a war, or a natural disaster! It takes so little for all our securities to go up in smoke at any moment. Let's attach ourselves to things which do not pass away, those which the god, modernism, cannot obtain for us. Let's attach ourselves to things that we can keep and taste for all eternity!

From the very depths of our souls, we all aspire to those realities which do not pass away. We are tired of spiritual gimmicks which leave us empty and with no future. We try in vain to deny eternity, but there's no way around it; we are created for eternity, and we are marked in the deepest part of ourselves with this thirst! And Maryam knew that well. By showing her the saints in that eternal beatitude, Our Lady set her soul on fire. She aimed straight for the heart, hit the bull's-eye, and unleashed the fire! Maryam's soul became like molten wax under the fire of the Holy Spirit, who enveloped her and penetrated her being. And onto this malleable wax, a kind of seal was stamped. For the rest of her days, Maryam would be marked with this seal, branded by this vision of heavenly things. From that time on, she couldn't help but live and suffer within the sphere of Heaven, eyes fixed eagerly on that future; and if she shared so well what she had seen, it is because she had been burned by this fire herself.

25. She retreated from nothing; fear was defeated

Yes, she was completely burned by that fire! So, I would like to pose a question here: What then, is this fire of love, which is so strong? So strong that Maryam would never again be afraid to face all the trials of this earth? She was so full of this fire, so transformed, that even martyrdom wouldn't frighten her! She wouldn't be afraid to endure illness! She wouldn't be afraid to speak the truth and allow herself to be scorned! She wouldn't be afraid to suffer a thousand deaths in order to win souls for God, through her prayers, through her sacrifices, through her offerings. She would retreat from nothing when it was a question of gaining souls for God, by the hundreds, by the thousands, and undoubtedly by the millions! Her joy would be to help souls recognize that happiness which she had simply had a glimpse of during her brief "visit" to heaven!

What did she end up telling us after all, our little Maryam? Quite simply: It exists! That happiness exists! It's there. It's already there! Only a sheer veil separates us from it. It exists, and it's on our doorstep. If only people would leave us alone with all these sceptic, depressing philosophies, all these shallow currents of thought limited to earthly concerns, all these atheistic and fallacious doctrines which abound in our era, and which would have us believe that there is nothing but the earth! That our journey ends in a deep black hole in the core of the earth! What a deadly bore!

Maryam tells us, together with Scripture, that eternity exists. In some ways, she reminds me of Saint Bernadette: She doesn't pose as a theoretician abounding in degrees. Instead, she comes to deliver to us a simple testimony about what her eyes saw and her heart experienced. She radiates with what she brings, and this brilliance is stronger than anything!

26. Visit from the souls in Purgatory

The result did not delay, it was so beautiful! The poor souls came to visit her, as she herself would say in her simple language. The happy souls of Heaven, as well as the souls of Purgatory would come to her and open themselves up to her with great familiarity.

Let's not forget that Maryam had seen Purgatory, and that there she received great illumination from God. This illumination was not only knowledge in itself or some kind of information to hold onto. No, it was, rather, a transforming light. All light which comes from God transforms the heart. Seeing those souls who suffered so much in Purgatory, Maryam developed a great compassion for them. She truly became attached to them. In this outpouring of her heart, she burned with a passionate desire to come to the aid of those souls who were suffering. It's not surprising then, that these souls should come in great numbers to visit her, all too happy to find someone so willing to help them!

Let's get back into some concrete examples. I'm thinking of a man, the father of a religious, who would later become part of the Carmelite community. This man had died an unbeliever. He had refused to the very end the sacraments and all help from the Church. Although he had been a good man on the whole, his life had not been a very glowing inspiration. So, this Carmelite nun had truly been anguished about the eternal fate of her father. Now, without her knowing it, her deceased father had come to visit Maryam to ask her to pray for him, because he was suffering in Purgatory. He explained that, in spite of his categorical refusal of the sacraments before dying, he had seen a light at the last moment, when his death had already been pronounced clinically. Thanks to that light, he had repented and had escaped Hell.

Maryam understood that one can never presume to know the final fate of a soul, because God alone sees into the depth of hearts at the moment of death. At that moment, God gives graces in great abundance, so that the soul will convert and turn towards Him, so that it will choose His light definitively. More than ever, at that very moment, we need to pray, we need to intercede for those souls!

This man explained to Maryam that he was in Purgatory, but that he had been able to be saved, thanks to that moment of repentance. But since he was still suffering in Purgatory, he came to ask for prayers. Maryam recounted that story to Mother Elie, who was the Carmelite daughter of this man. Mother Elie exclaimed: "But that's unbelievable, that whole story! I thank you, but if it is really from the Lord, tell me the name of my father!" Maryam answered: "His name is Reuch." That was indeed the name of Mother Elie's father, a fact no one knew. In that way, the Carmelite had proof that Maryam had been visited by this man from Purgatory. Since he had asked that several Masses be celebrated in his favor and that people make novenas of prayers, those things were done. At the end of those Masses and novenas, he returned to visit Maryam to say: "It is done. I have now entered Heaven!"

27. A very expensive 5 francs coin!

Here is another example: The soul of a nun came to find Maryam, because she had been truly plunged into the depths of pain in Purgatory. And she explained why: "When I was on Earth, I was in a religious community. Now, I had secretly hidden a coin of five francs in a little nook, in case the community was ever in need, in case we might lack something; and this was without the knowledge of my superiors. Right to the end, I wouldn't give it up." So, on this nun's part, there was not only dissimulation, but also a lack of poverty, despite the fact that she had taken the vow of poverty, of total detachment. There was also this stubbornness, because, even on her death bed, she wouldn't admit her fault! Since she had been a long time in Purgatory, she asked for prayers from Maryam. The most incredible thing was that she indicated to Maryam where that five-franc coin could be found (that was a large sum at the time!). The Sisters conducted a search and found it!

It is through these very concrete things that the Lord came to instruct Maryam. She realized during these moments in what a sad state those souls were arriving before God, still bound, still attached to certain wilful sins or to certain weaknesses.

28. Unfortunate damages of bitterness

Another revealing example: Again, it involves a nun. Before entering the convent, she belonged to a very rich family, and she had significant personal possessions. On the other hand, her religious community was very poor. Now this Sister had ambition and tried to secure the position of prioress. When she was not elected to that position by her Sisters, she formed a plan to avenge herself on them. At the moment of deciding to whom her possessions would go, instead of giving them to her community, which was in need, she insisted on giving them to her family, which was rich, not so much out of love for her family but out of spite, because she hadn't been elected prioress. After many years had passed, she was able to get hold of herself and ask for forgiveness, but she had harbored this bitterness throughout her entire life as a religious, and she had died in these sentiments of bitter self-love, without repenting of having acted in this way. She was suffering, therefore, in Purgatory because of that and came one day to Maryam to plead for the help of her prayers for a quick liberation.

Another example, that of a religious: Throughout her life, she appeared to be a saint around her Sisters. Since she was thought a saint, people didn't pray much for the salvation of her soul. In fact, the worst service one can render to the deceased is to canonize them too early, thus depriving them of prayers of intercession from which they could benefit. It's terrible! This Sister came, then, to ask help from Maryam, explaining to her that, under the guise of holiness, she had secretly turned her Sisters against their superiors, then had died with these feelings of rebellion towards her superiors. She said to Maryam: "A person who rebels against her superiors, rebels against God." From the depths of Purgatory, she came to implore help. It would have been so simple to repent before death!

Another example: A woman explained to Maryam that she had come very close to Hell. But she had been saved thanks only to the prayers of her children, and, of course, to the mercy of God. Her children had prayed greatly for her, and, thanks to their intercession, she had escaped eternal separation from God, in other words, Hell. She explained to Maryam why, without them, she would have deserved Hell. Because throughout her life, she had sought only to do her own will.

A further example: A soul from Purgatory visited Maryam, and this woman had led a rather mediocre and luke-warm life, in a word she had not overexerted herself for the Lord. She wanted to tell Maryam that she had just gotten out of Purgatory and entered Heaven, because at one time, she had given a large gift to the Church, while participating in the construction of a Basilica. It was on the very day of the dedication of this Basilica that she was able to leave Purgatory and enter Heaven. The Lord had remembered this generous gift from her!

29. *Splendid origin, splendid destiny*

We can guess what some people are saying to themselves: "What's with all these stories?! Heaven, Purgatory, Hell... All these are tales from ages past! We're beyond all that!"

First of all, we should not link Purgatory with the notion of punishment by God, still less with chastisement. In reality, God is nothing but love and mercy, and it is His mercy which invented Purgatory!

But let's go back to basics: we are all made for God. We are created to enter into an extremely pure relationship with Him, a loving relationship. Our time on Earth is given to us specifically in order to work on our own conversion, to work at the things of the Kingdom, and to grow in this union of love. More often than not, we occupy ourselves with many other things and forget that we have an immortal soul! As Mary says in Medjugorje, "You occupy yourselves with many things, but the soul is the least of them." By doing this, we delay our purification while God, on His part, gives us every opportunity we need on earth to be sufficiently pure to appear before Him. Saint John of the Cross tells us in essence that if we accept all the opportunities that God gives us on earth to purify ourselves, the trials and even the penances that He inspires in us, if we welcome them with gratitude towards the Lord (and not bitterness), we are sure to go straight to Heaven. The trials that He offers take the place of Purgatory for us."

30. Why don't many souls go straight to Heaven?

It's because we complain, we grumble, we moan, we struggle against the Lord. We aren't happy. We protest against the cross. Sometimes we even blaspheme when facing a trial. We occupy ourselves with things other than the glory of God. We have other ambitions. When the hour of death arrives, we are not purified; we have missed the opportunities! So, in His extreme mercy, the Lord adds more time, a delay of sorts, a new opportunity to purify ourselves, a kind of middle stage between Earth and Heaven, and that is Purgatory.

In Purgatory, what purifies us is neither the punishment of the Lord, nor the suffering in itself. What purifies us is love. The fire of love! Everyone meets God at the moment of his death. Out of love for Him, we are overwhelmed with extreme sorrow at having loved Him so little on Earth. It is a suffering of love, a loving nostalgia. Purgatory is a place of great love! These souls suffer from devouring desire to con-template Infinite Love. The souls who find themselves there would not want for the world to return to Earth. The souls of Purgatory are happy to be saved, they are sure of their eterni-ty of happiness. They know that they will be with God forever, and that certitude gives them joy in the midst of suffering. However, Purgatory is also a place in the dark night, because they do not yet see this Beloved God. Now the absence of that vision brings pain, more pain than the greatest physical suffering on Earth, according to the mystics. To not see Him, even for a short while, that is torture! Those in great love can understand that. No longer to see the loved one, when they have already tasted his ineffable love, is an agony for the heart.

We need the Maryams, Catherines of Siena, Sister Faustinas, we need witnesses, privileged by God and graced by extraordinary heavenly visits, to remind us that these souls in Purgatory are waiting eagerly for our prayers! In fact, through prayer, we can hasten the end of that suffering for our loved ones, for those who have gone before us. It is sufficient, for example, to offer an hour of adoration of the Blessed Sacrament or to have a Mass said, for a soul to be freed from the suffering of Purgatory. Vicka Ivankovic, the visionary of Medjugorje who has seen Purgatory, said to me: "If you saw even once those souls who are suffering, you would not forget for a single day to pray for them. You would want to empty Purgatory!" Pope John Paul II recalls it in his great exhortation for the Holy Year of 2000 that, through our prayers, we have the power to hasten the eternal happiness of those who are dear to us and of all souls who are waiting eagerly for Heaven.

Maryam, in her great compassion for those who suffer, used this power to the fullest, right up until her final breath! Today, from the highest Heaven, it goes without saying that her intercession has grown in power! Why not profit from it and have the Church profit from it?

31. Maryam at Marseille

Let's follow up, briefly, on the historical account of her life. We find her again at age 19 at Marseille, living with the Sisters of Saint Joseph. She was assigned to the kitchen as an aide to the cook, charged with the simplest but hardest tasks. God permitted that her companion in the kitchen be a nun who was particularly nasty. She gave her a hard time, humiliated her in a thousand ways and accused her of things falsely. Faced with all that, Maryam remained a model of patience, forgiveness, charity, and self-effacement.

32. The stigmata

It was also at this time that the stigmata appeared on her body. With regard to the stigmata, I would like to insist on one point. She received them during prayer, so that she would hold in her hand an image of Jesus crucified. She would pray while looking at this image and be filled with compassion and love towards Jesus, who suffered on the cross. So, God permitted these wounds to be imprinted on the body of Maryam. I would like to emphasize this aspect of compassionate prayer on the part of Maryam. Stigmata are extraordinary signs of a profoundly mystical life. But mystical life does not consist in these visible and extraordinary phenomena. Mystical life consists in the union of the soul with the Lord.

There are great mystics who are not detectable by others. The Lord hides them from the eyes of men. Their souls are profoundly united with the Lord's, and they show no visible sign of extraordinary phenomena. For Maryam, it was, above all, her heart which was deeply united to the Lord's, but Jesus wanted to imprint these exterior and visible signs on the body of His spouse, to signify the union of His heart with hers.

33. The transverberation

Throughout Maryam's life, it was this union of her heart with Christ's which would prevail. A little later, she would even experience the grace of "transverberation." That is a rare grace that some saints have received (for example, Saint Teresa of Avila, Saint Catherine of Sienna, and so on). Jesus Himself comes to pierce the heart of His disciple, imprinting on him His own piercing. From then on, it is no longer the heart of the saint which beats in his chest, but the actual Heart of Jesus. For Maryam, the extreme charity which burned in her heart truly came from the charity of the Heart of Christ.

It was from there, from that source of love that all the rest emanated. There she was, then, marked with the stigmata, and she was also seized more and more frequently with what are called "ecstasies."

34. The ecstasies

According to the testimony of the Carmelites of Bethlehem, Maryam spent hours, and sometimes entire days in ecstasy, keeping company with the Lord, contemplating Him in the midst of the world, in souls, in heaven, everywhere that He is present. At those moments, she was also uniting herself to His suffering, to His desires, to His prayers, all the while losing consciousness of the outside world which surrounded her.

God permitted her to be unconscious of all these exterior mystical manifestations. Each time she was forced to take note of the fact, for example, that she had spent three hours in ecstasy and that she had missed saying the Divine Office, or recreation, or a meal, she was very confused about it, and she did everything to hide it. When she had to explain her absences, she didn't say, "I was having an ecstasy," but "I was taking a nap," and she asked her mother superior to "keep me from falling asleep." That meant: "Keep me from falling into ecstasy." She was very confused and even humiliated about doing things differently from others. That mark of humility was a sign of the authenticity of her heart, in the midst of all these mystical manifestations.

When the day arrived for her to take the habit of the Sisters of Saint Joseph, it was decided that she just couldn't do it. Basically, her superiors found that she displayed too many qualities which did not completely conform to the apostolic vocation of the Sisters of St. Joseph. She was too mystical in a way. The council of Sisters decided, therefore, not to keep her but to direct her towards a more contemplative life.

35. The Carmelite convent in Pau

Maryam was 20 years old when she left the Sisters of Saint Joseph to enter the Carmelite convent at Pau (near Lourdes) in France. From the moment of her arrival at this convent, she felt completely at home. She very much appreciated the cloister, the silence, the life of mortification and of humility, and all those practices of obedience which played such an important part.

Immediately, she felt in the deepest part of her being how much this vocation of a Carmelite suited her. She was going to try to be what was called a "choir Sister." But, because of her ignorance, her fundamental incapacity to learn the liturgy, to read, to write, to study, she found herself unable to chant the office and was eventually given the role of "converse Sister." To be a "converse Sister" consisted of taking care of all the heavy duties of the monastery (kitchen, garden, laundry, repairs etc) and also buying supplies needed by the community. She was in contact with the outside world. She would be like the angel, the servant of the monastery.

It was at the convent in Pau that a very important event in Maryam's life occurred. She would actually confront the Evil One in a very particular way. We will see this a little later on.

36. Founding of the convent at Mangalore

The Sisters of the convent in Pau decided to start a Carmelite convent in the Indies. It was Monsignor Mary Ephrem, a Carmelite priest, whose diocese was at that time in the Indies, who asked for a convent of Carmelites. Sister Mary of Jesus Crucified was to be among those who departed for that place. The journey was very, very rough, and three Sisters would perish along the way. At that time, such a voyage took months! In order to get to such a faraway place, one had to face so many risks: hunger, drowning, epidemics, pirates, etc. Sister Maryam would escape these misfortunes and be among the founders of this convent in the city of Mangalore.

It was in the Carmelite convent in Mangalore that she would make her final vows.

37. Interior martyrdom

It was also in this convent that our newly professed Sister would endure a terrible trial. If, at the convent in Pau, she enjoyed the love of her Sisters and their esteem, the Lord had other plans for her time in Mangalore. He permitted her to be plunged into a terrible suffering, one of those sufferings which He Himself had known on earth: the pain of being rejected by His own people, and particularly by those leaders of her own religion.

Imagine Jesus, accused of blasphemy by the High Priests and all the Sanhedrin. Imagine Jesus, wounded by the exclusion of his own people and condemned to death! Sister Mary of Jesus Crucified, whose name signifies a particular union with the passion of Christ, was going to enter into this interior martyrdom. It was her vocation. She was going to undergo this same trial: to be banished, to be wounded by exclusion, to be seemingly deleted from the Book of Life.

So, it happened that within several months, her entire community, the mother superior herself, even the bishop of that area, all declared that Sister Mary of Jesus Crucified was living in spiritual delusion and that her words came from the Devil. They were sincerely convinced that it was Satan who inspired her. So, she was sent back from the convent at Mangalore, like a victim of the plague!

38. The light finally comes!

It is worth noting that, from the depths of her heart, in these dark hours, Maryam remained in profound peace. She returned, therefore, to the convent in Pau. After this trial that she had undergone with enormous heroism, the winds changed for her, and in a good direction this time. The Lord, who had permitted this temporary blindness on the part of her superiors, allowed the light to shine through at last. The Prioress of the convent at Mangalore, enlightened by the Holy Spirit, wrote a letter to the convent in Bethlehem and to Sister Mary of Jesus Crucified to explain the enlightenment which she had received and to ask for forgiveness. She declared humbly that she was mistaken, that she had wanted to do the right thing, but that she had been blinded. She withdrew all the negative judgments which had been pronounced against Maryam. So, the truth triumphed in the end. Maryam was rehabilitated and her reputation restored. She could once more live in peace in her Carmelite convent, welcomed by her Sisters and by the entire community.

If the Lord permitted this trial for Maryam, it was with the goal of testing her and making her grow. He also wanted to fortify His little spouse and prepare her to found another convent. Yes, the founding of a new Carmelite convent would be entrusted by God to Maryam.

39. Plans designed in Heaven?

Maryam actually received the inspiration to found two Carmelite convents in Palestine. A very strange thing! In fact, at the end of the 19th century, Palestine had a Turkish government, and absolutely no one could envision the founding of a contemplative monastery. It was completely out of the question. But Maryam received from the Lord Jesus the explicit command to found two Carmelite convents, first of all one in Bethlehem, and later on another one in Nazareth. The Lord specifically said "in the cradle of my father David." Here, something totally unique took place: seven times Jesus entered the cell of Maryam and showed her the monastery of Bethlehem, which she was charged with building!

It's very beautiful. Imagine Jesus appearing in Maryam's cell on seven occasions to show her how to construct this monastery! Jesus showed her the whole monastery and then He opened it before her eyes so that she may see the inside of it. It was in the shape of a circle contained within a garden. Maryam tried to sketch the plans with the help of others. She had all the measurements and all the details which she gave to Father Bordachar who drew the final plan according to the will of Our Lord. The monastery had the shape of a tower but also of a star whose chapel and outbuildings are like the rays that emanate from the star. Jesus explained to Maryam how to obtain authorization for it from Rome, how to inform the patriarch, etc. The obtaining of that permission was a succession of little miracles. In a word, Heaven and earth have co-operated in the building of this monastery.

40. A watch tower

Maryam was then sent out with several Sisters to the Holy Land to establish this monastery. I must point out that this convent in Bethlehem still exists today. I have visited it several times. It is constructed like a tower, like a very imposing fortress. The Lord had indicated quite well the reason: it had to be a place of combat, a place where the Sister would have to struggle against the powers of evil, in order to bring back the victory of light, and this for all the souls who are consecrated mystically to the Carmelites. So, this kind of citadel, of watch tower, if I may call it that, with its ramparts and its extremely high, thick walls is a sign of that vocation.

When you go to the Holy Land, don't miss visiting this Carmelite convent!

As the Lord indicated, this convent is built on the very place where David kept his sheep. Beneath the convent you can still see the grotto where David received from the prophet Samuel the anointing of the Lord, the holy oil which made him king of Israel, (1 Sam 16: 2-13). It is a place of rich blessings, of course. This place is found on the side of a hill. According to what Jesus revealed to Maryam, it is also the place where His parents, Joseph and Mary, stopped for a while to pray, wanting to rest a bit before going down into the village to find lodging for the birth of their child.

It is truly the Old and the New Testaments which are joined on this humble hill! Jesus promised Maryam that this convent would be kept intact until He came in glory. Few monasteries have received such a promise from Heaven! Knowing that, I examined closely the construction of this convent: it is solid and robust with thick foundation walls, and it has already remained intact for more than a century! And I asked myself how much longer would it be able to stand? A long time, obviously! It is a durable work, conceived by a divine architect and built by a saint.

41. Jesus and Maryam collaborate on the work

What is also striking in this convent is to see with what simplicity the Lord has taken care of each detail. He had specified to Maryam that the convent should be poor. The prioress (the one I met in 1983) says that it is actually a little too small, that it lacks space. I believe that Jesus did this on purpose, so that the Sisters would partake of His own poverty on Earth. The curves are very gentle, very humane. All the doors are rather low and vaulted, like the ones of the first century of our era, the ones Jesus was familiar with, as though he made them with his own carpenter's hands! The proportions exude harmony.

Maryam directed the construction, and, when the Arab workers made a little addition to the right or to the left (The Arabs are crazy about flourishes!), the Lord would come to find Maryam and tell her: "They have added a molding in such and such a corner. Have it taken off!" Jesus was very strict when it came to the actualization of His plan. This collaboration between Jesus and Maryam is very moving, unique! It is simply overwhelming to enter this convent and to remind yourself that it was Jesus who inspired the blue prints! We are discovering a little about Jesus' tastes!

The chapel of the Sisters also struck me. For example, the base of the windows is over your head if you are standing. There, also, we see a lesson from Jesus: a Carmelite, in prayer, should be thinking only of Heaven. You can see neither trees, nor houses, nor even the surrounding hills. You see only the sky. A Carmelite in her prayer ought to be occupied only with the things of Heaven, and she ought to, by her life and her prayer, direct the entire world towards Heaven. There! This whole convent is conceived like that, and one finds there a source rich with teachings!

42. Her time is getting short

Sister Mary of Jesus Crucified remained for about three years in the convent of Bethlehem, in order to take charge of construction. There she pursued her ministry of intercession, her ministry of offering herself for the world, with great joy and great suffering in her body and in her soul, in union with Christ. But she lived through all of it in peace. She had a reputation for good humor, for joy and spontaneity. She was known for always giving words of comfort, words of hope, which her Sisters needed, even in the midst of the worst difficulties. She was radiant!

But her time was short, and according to her own prediction, she would die at the age of 32. One day, when she was directing construction on the monastery, she fell in a small stairway. She was seriously wounded, and gangrene took over her arm. An incurable disease in this era, at the end of the 19th century. And our dear Maryam would die of this gangrene, to which we must add exhaustion and all the physical ailments that she accumulated during the course of her brief existence. Maryam died proclaiming the mercy of

God, like Jesus. Let's say, rather, that she was born into Heaven! To be precise, she died on August 26, 1878, as another great Carmelite nun, St. Thérèse of the Child Jesus, was barely 4 years old.

II. Maryam, the Little Prophet

Let's tackle now the important points of Maryam's message, because these are a gold mine, pure illuminations for our times. The Lord permitted this message to remain in the shadows for 100 years, and it is not by chance that it comes into the light of day now, because our generation needs it more than ever!

I can't help but begin with a message from Maryam which concerns the Holy Spirit and is addressed particularly to the Church. We know that in the 19th century, devotion to the Holy Spirit was not predominant in the Catholic Church, far from it! Now, Maryam lived from the Holy Spirit.

43. Come, my Consolation!

According to the testimony of her Sisters, she had an extraordinary devotion to the Holy Spirit, and she had this prayer on her lips at all times:

"Holy Spirit, inspire me. Love of God, consume me. Along the right path, guide me. Mary, my Mother, look down upon me. With Jesus, bless me. From all harm, all illusion, all danger, preserve me."

Maryam called upon the Holy Spirit in all places and all circumstances. She called upon Him with all her heart. As soon as there was a decision to make, a choice to make, as soon as there was a problem to solve, she invoked the Holy Spirit. She truly called upon Him in every circumstance imaginable.

She called Him with the words of a child: "Come, my Consolation, my Joy, come my Peace, my Strength, my Light. Come! Show me where to find the Spring which will quench my thirst." She called Him without ceasing; she truly lived in Him. It must be said that Maryam was very conscious of being the least of the ignorant, so much so that she was actually suspended to the light of the Holy Spirit. Without the Holy Spirit to enlighten her about Jesus and about the mysteries of the faith, she would know nothing. That is why she called upon Him without ever letting up. She said, "The Holy Spirit refuses me nothing, the Holy Spirit refuses me nothing."

44. The Holy Spirit refuses me nothing

So, she gave to the entire Church a model for living from the Holy Spirit. Actually, she received from the Lord a very specific directive that is valid for the whole Church.

Here is the message that Maryam transmits to us (It is Jesus who is speaking to her): "Whoever invokes the Holy Spirit, will look for Me and find Me. His conscience will be as delicate as a flower in the field. If the person is the father or mother of a family, peace will reign in his family, and his heart will be in peace in this world and in the next. He will not die in darkness, but in peace."

Here is the part of the message intended for priests: "I ardently desire that priests say a Mass each month in honor of the Holy Spirit. Whoever says that Mass or hears it will be honored by the Holy Spirit Himself. He will have light; he will have peace. He will cure the sick. He will awaken those who sleep."

What an awesome message! What a splendid promise from the Lord! Maryam would transmit it to her bishop, asking him on the part of the Lord to transmit it to the Holy Father, who was at that time Pope Pius XI.

45. No one will believe me!

Let's note here an interesting fact: at the dawn of the 20th century, that is, on the night of December 31, 1899 and January 1, 1900, a little after the death of Maryam, Pope Leo XIII consecrated the entire Church to the Holy Spirit. It wouldn't surprise anyone if the prayer of Maryam and her petitions addressed to Rome weren't among the motivations which pushed Leo XIII to make this consecration! (Even before this, Pope Leo XIII in his letter Provida Mater (May 5, 1895) and in his encyclical, Divinum illum munus (May 9, 1897), answered the plea of Maryam, prescribing the novena to the Holy Spirit as a preparation to the feast of Pentecost).

When Jesus confided this message to Maryam, she answered: "But I, Lord, what can I do? If I say that, no one will believe me." But Jesus reassured her: "When the moment comes, I will do it all Myself, and it will have nothing to do with you."

What struck Sister Maryam of Jesus Crucified was that this grace was offered to every soul: the grace to allow oneself to be inspired by the Holy Spirit. She loved to repeat: "We have a Holy Spirit!" and she was always pained to see that the world and even certain members of the Church, lived as if the Holy Spirit didn't exist.

For example, in the case of religious communities whose deficiencies she saw, along with the pain that they caused the Lord, she would say: "The world and religious communities are looking for novelties in their devotions and are neglecting the true devotion to the Paraclete; that is why there is error and disunity, and why there is neither peace nor light." Maryam stressed that, in these communities and among Christians, people did not call for divine illumination as much as it ought to be called for. She would say: "It is this light of the Holy Spirit which allows us to know the truth. Even in seminaries, people neglect this devotion to the Holy Spirit."

This essential deficiency was for her a source of great suffering. Every day, she experienced the fact that with the Holy Spirit one had all that was necessary to live in the light, and she never understood how anyone could pass up this gift from God.

46. Why is the world in darkness?

She used to say: "Within religious orders, persecutions reign; jealousy rules among the religious orders, and that is why the world is in darkness." Because the religious, the consecrated souls, the priests, are precisely the ones who have received this call to beckon the Holy Spirit to earth, they bear a great responsibility. If they neglect to invoke the Holy Spirit, the entire world is plunged into darkness. And already, Maryam had the intuition that things were going to degrade further in times to come. Jesus revealed to her that there would be much defection in religious orders, among the priests, and that this would bring darkness over the entire world. Recalling the souls who did not know God, Jesus told her that these souls would be plunged into darkness because of these defections. Maryam suffered immensely over this, in communion with Christ.

She used to say, "No person, in the world or in these communities, who invokes the Holy Spirit and has this devotion, will die in error." In our century, when so many people no longer know which way to go, when confusion of spirit reigns in so many areas, Maryam shows us a very simple solution, received from the Lord Himself in Scripture: "The Paraclete will remind you of all I have told you." There are not a thousand other solutions; it is the Holy Spirit who will enlighten us, and we received Him on Pentecost.

As for the priests, she expresses great hope, "Every priest who preaches this devotion will receive the light while he is speaking to others." These are most precious words!

47. *Unraveling the schemes of Satan*

Another point in the message of Maryam seems to me very strong, because it touches upon the means used by Satan, about whom our present world is all too silent. In order to bring back a victory in spiritual combat, it is essential to know not only the identity of the enemy, but also his tactics and his way of acting. That permits us to take up the appropriate weapons to defeat him. I found this testimony in the book by Father Estrate, Maryam's spiritual director, who received her confidences.

During her stay in the Carmelite convent in Pau, Maryam lived through a trial similar to the one of Job, recounted in the Book of Job. One day, God gave permission to Satan to try His servant Job, who gave Him such beautiful devotion. Satan lost no time in submitting Job to some very difficult trials. He tested his fidelity by cruelly stripping him of everything except his life, in order to push him into blasphemy. But the fidelity of Job to God remained intact, and Satan failed totally in his plan of destruction. Even after this "visit from the Evil One," Job was seven times more blessed than before, in his life, in his worldly goods, as well as in his personal character. Now, Satan did the same for Maryam: he went to God in order to obtain from Him permission to try her very harshly, to tempt her and even to "possess" her for forty days. Happily, we have the account of this trial, thanks to the presence of witnesses around Maryam during those days. That account is infinitely precious to us, because the Lord allowed Maryam to unveil the schemes of Satan. A gripping story!

48. The 40-day trial

Satan, the adversary par excellence, was furious to see all the souls whom this "little Arab" (He called her that) snatched away from him. By the thousands, she snatched these souls out of darkness to offer them to God. We are going to witness a truly gripping confrontation between the Evil One and Maryam. Satan imposed a real torture on Maryam. But she got through all these interior and corporal sufferings with great faithfulness to God, and through constant prayer.

Here are several bits of dialogue overheard by the Sisters at the convent and by a few priests who were present during this trial.

Right from the start, Satan explained his rage by saying, "This wretched Arab, I will break her! The older she gets, the more my rage builds up, especially because of those marks." (When Satan says "those marks," he means the stigmata that Maryam bore on her body). Then God compelled Satan to uncover the schemes he used to ruin religious souls. Let's be attentive to these revelations; we'll profit from them a great deal!

49. How many religious souls we take into our ranks!

Satan began to boast, saying, "There! I just brought down a nun in England! She's been ours since the day before yesterday." Then he explained his tactics, his usual tactics. "When we lay siege to a soul consecrated to God, we begin by tempting her in little things.

Then we get her to believe that she is not loved by her superior to the same degree as the others. She begins to feel jealousy, and that leads her to write letters in secret. Then she ends up wanting to leave." Oh, how many souls in religious life we take into our ranks by suggesting to them the thought that no one thinks they are good at anything! That no one loves them! Then we win others through the desire to see and to know everything." Then Satan adds these words heavy with meaning: "Triumphing over a soul who has pronounced the three bad words (meaning the three vows), is for us more than being mayor of an entire city." That explains the capital interest the Evil One has in ruining in particular those souls consecrated to God.

As a matter of fact, the spiritual stakes entrusted to the consecrated life are enormous for all the other souls. As a small aside, here are some words from the Lord to Maryam which clarify this idea: "If, in a city, even one completely perverted, I find one soul, a single soul who is faithful to his vows, I will save the entire city." We can see what hinges on a single soul who is faithful to God! That isn't something new, it's a biblical truth. A beautiful example is given to us in the book of Genesis during the compelling dialogue between God and Abraham. Abraham intercedes with God so that He will not destroy the city of Sodom, as He has planned. Abraham tells Him that there are, perhaps, some righteous in the city, and that He couldn't, therefore, destroy the righteous with the sinners. (Gen.18: 16-33)

Do you also remember the episode recounted by Jeremiah (Jer.11: 13)? God is complaining to his prophet because of Jerusalem:

"For your gods have become as many as your cities... and as many as the streets of Jerusalem are the altars you have set up to shame, altars to burn incense to Ba'al." A little later, the Lord says that if He found in Jerusalem a single just soul, He would save the entire city. What a monumental lesson for us! If we are faithful to our commitments, to our total gift of self to the Lord, the Lord will save many souls, and even entire cities!

50. To offer oneself to the point of martyrdom

Maryam adds on the part of Jesus, that "He who follows the Rule in full has the crown of martyrdom." Because to be faithful to one's vows, to be faithful to the Rule of the community and to its spirit, is truly to offer oneself to the point of martyrdom. The person is already a martyr inside. It is through this martyrdom of love that the Lord can save multitudes of souls. The Evil One explains clearly his rage against consecrated souls and his desire to triumph over them. So, in this battle that the Evil One undertook against Maryam, his goal was to push her to complain just a single time of the suffering he made her endure, and he declared loudly: "I'm going to get one single complaint out of her."

You see the heroism of Maryam during those forty days! In her extreme charity, she accepted suffering all those tribulations, all that suffering, in order to offer them to Christ, in union with His own, for the redemption of souls. It is in that, more than in anything, that we see how much Maryam burned with charity. It is only charity, the fire of true charity that could have enabled her to undergo and to offer up all those sufferings without complaining.

The Evil One, as hard as he tried in every way during those forty days, didn't obtain a single complaint, not a single one! He didn't even succeed in getting her to say simply, "I'm suffering, I can't do it anymore." On the contrary, each time she "came to" (she was rendered mute most of the time because of this possession), what did she say? "Lord, I offer you all this pain for the Church, for the holiness of priests, for souls in distress, for souls who are lost," etc.

51. Weapons to conquer Satan

This succession of uninterrupted victories by the young novice always diminished the forces of Satan and covered him with confusion. Understanding that he was losing in every way, he began to beg the Lord to be able to stop the fight. He regretted having proposed this "deal," and he wanted to renege on his decision. But what did the Lord reply to him? "You asked me to put her body to the test for forty days: you will not get out of it until after the 40 days." The devil found himself obliged to go to the very end of those forty days, even though he was losing more each day.

Every person present could hear the peaceful voice of Maryam: "I unite myself to Jesus and Mary. I offer my suffering for those who are against the Church. Blessed be my God!" Instead of complaints, it was blessings that Maryam addressed to God.

So, Satan continued, under orders from the Lord, to reveal to Maryam and to her whole community his sordid tactics and things about himself. He said, for example: "The three most powerful things against us are charity, humility, and obedience." He added, "I am the Tempter. I sow division everywhere. I do what I want." We see here the dangers of self-will, as opposed to Jesus who said to His Father: "Not My will, but Your will be done." Another thing: Satan takes off the veil of a Sister, saying: "I am taking off this veil, because I do not like modesty. It irritates me."

Another example: He publicly accused Maryam of her sins. You know, the Evil One is the Accuser (this is how St. John defined him in the Book of Revelation). So, he accused Maryam, but what did she reply? "Yes, I am nothing but sin, but I hope in the mercy of God." Then the devil cried out: "A little nobody will triumph over us, that's impossible!"

Maryam explained to him that even if he had the power to torture her and break her temporarily, he did only what the Master permitted. We find here the very words of Sister Faustina Kowalska, forty years later:

She was walking towards her convent when demons barred her path. "They were threatening me with terrible tortures," she wrote, and voices were heard: "She has taken away all that we worked for, for so many years!' "Seeing their terrible hatred towards me, I called upon my Guardian Angel right away for help, and immediately his clear and radiant appearance stood near me. And he said to me, "Have no fear, Spouse of my Lord; without His permission, these spirits will do you no harm." Immediately the evil spirits disappeared and my faithful Guardian Angel accompanied me in person up to the house." (Diary, §419).

Satan could do nothing without the permission of God. He was obliged to obey!

52. She carries off victory after victory

So, the devil was forced to reveal the cause of his defeat: "Do you know why the little Arab speaks this way? Why she is strong? Because she walks in the footsteps of the Master." Let's remember the words of Jesus, who says, "I am the light of the world. He who follows Me will not walk in darkness but will have the light of life." That is really the bond Maryam has with Jesus. It is her conforming to the Lord Jesus which permits her, in all serenity, to carry off victory after victory over Satan. She walks in the footsteps of the Master and that is why she is strong.

In fact, all possible temptations passed through her, one after the other, because Satan was taking advantage of the situation. At one particular moment, Maryam said, "Satan, are you tempting me against the Church? I love the Church. She is my mother; she will crush your head. My Mother the Church will not fall. It is you, Satan, who will fall. You fell once from Heaven, and ever since then you have continued to fall." She added, "If men saw you, they would never follow you. You miserable wretch, people don't see you until death. If they could only see your face, the whole world would run from you."

She added, also, "Satan, you fell in full light: we fall from weakness. Whoever follows the light has a righteous heart. You seek to trick souls. Jesus seeks to lift them up. Me, I am nobody. Through Jesus, I will be above you. Jesus will be my light. Jesus chose the weak. Because I am weak, He has chosen me."

Each time Maryam regained her spirits in the middle of her suffering, she would say: "Glory to Jesus! Glory to Jesus!" The furious demon would say, "What is she saying, this Arab? Is it possible? No, no, glory to me! Glory to me!"

Then Maryam would say: "When the Spirit of God comes down into a soul, He brings calm, peace and joy. When it is you, Satan, you bring only anxiety, pain, and trouble." She would add, "When God wants something, you can't do anything to change it. You have to obey Jesus, trembling in your boots."

53. High places where eternity is at stake

You see this kind of trial and this extraordinary dialogue between a child of light and the Prince of Darkness? It gives us a keen understanding of the dimension of spiritual combat, which is in the process of flaring up, and of its stakes. What are these stakes? Each of our souls, and all the souls of all time!

In this crucial episode of her life, Maryam seemed to become the target of a desperate persecution by the one who works day and night to ruin us. But it is absolutely clear that, at that moment, she did her job as a Carmelite. She stayed true to her consecration. For those who think that behind the walls of a Carmelite convent, nothing ever happens, that this existence behind the grilled screens is only time wasted, energy lost, what a mistake!

In reality, these Carmelites and all religious communities faithful to their vocations, are high places where eternities are played out. We must give thanks for this almost indiscreet peek into the tiny cell of Maryam, so well hidden in her convent, because this revelation comes at the right time, at an hour when, more than ever, The Evil One is increasing his devastation. In fact, we are almost relieved to see that all the evil that happens in the world does not come from our psyches or from our deficient natures, but that it comes from a real enemy, and that this enemy is a person who has a name.

54. It is Satan who is afraid of us

Yes, this is really a question of someone who comes to attack us, an angelic person, with his own personality, and not a sort of negative energy which floats in the air, without personality, as some dubious spiritualities of our time suggest. It is of utmost importance to understand that this someone, in fact, is the person who is afraid! It is Satan who is afraid of us when, in order to defeat him, we take up the weapons of Jesus; that is, humility, obedience, love. It is he, Satan, who trembles with fear in front of a soul who abandons himself to love! A person who lives with Jesus in truth has not the tiniest fear of Satan. This is the example and the lesson that Maryam delivers to us through her life.

We see, then, that to bring back victory in spiritual battle, Maryam used three weapons in particular: first of all, that of humility. With regard to humility, she emphasized several essential points. I would like to cite some of them in the hope that our lives can be enlightened.

She used to say, "Pride, everything infuriates it, everything annoys it, everything angers it, brings it down. Pride, everything revolts it, everything distresses it. It has anguish in this world and in the next. Humility has joy in this world and in the next."

Do you remember those words of the Blessed Mother when she took care of Maryam, lying lifeless in the grotto with her throat slit? When Our Lady nourished her with a mysterious and delicious soup and taught her about the spiritual life? At that moment, she gave her this priceless advice: "Always be content!"

Throughout the spiritual battles of Maryam, it is precisely on this point that Satan would attack her. He would do anything to force her to complain, to rebel against her suffering, against her fate, and even against the will of God for her. In short, he wanted to communicate to her his own feelings of frustration.

55. Humility is happy in everything

Now Our Lady taught Maryam the opposite attitude: "Always be content!" That is, welcome everything as coming from the hand of God, accept everything! That is what humility is. "Humility," says Maryam, "doesn't get upset about anything; it is content with everything." In order to mold His little spouse, the Lord spoke to her in parables. "Look at the earthworm. As long as it stays underground, it is safe: but if it shows itself, it will be crushed." Maryam tells us, "Humility is the kingdom of God's heart. Humility is satisfied with everything. Humility carries the Lord everywhere in his heart. It is God who gives the sincere humility of the heart. But you have to act. When there is true humility, you don't worry about the esteem, the judgment, or the regard of others."

Then, Jesus showed her Hell and said, "There are in Hell all kinds of virtues, but there is no humility. In Heaven, there are all kinds of faults, but no pride."

Maryam also described humility in this brilliantly concise way: "Happy the little ones! There is room for them everywhere. But the big ones, they get in everyone's way." She declared that nothing pleased the Lord more than humility. The Lord said to her, "Give me a priest or religious who has humility, and I will refuse him nothing." That's a powerful phrase to remember: "I will refuse him nothing!"

On the subject of sin in the world, let's listen to this dialogue between Jesus and Maryam: The Lord says,

- Give me a priest, find a single one, who is seeking only Me and who seeks nothing for himself. Who doesn't go out of his way to make beautiful speeches simply for the effect those speeches might have.

—But Lord, answers Maryam, there are still holy priests on this earth!

—If there could be found a single one, completely disengaged from himself, who looks only for the glory of God, that priest would do prodigious things. Miracles would spring from his hands.

That's the promise that Jesus gave Maryam, and surely to each of us! Oh, the power of humility!

The second weapon that Maryam proposes, and that she uses herself in this battle against darkness, is obedience. She practices obedience to the point of heroism. How can we not think here of Jesus and His agony at Gethsemane? He was assailed by anguish, distress, mortal sadness and by terrible interior suffering. All of Hell was in league against Him, exteriorly and interiorly. Now, it was at that precise moment that He pronounced the words of obedience par excellence: "Father, not my will but Thine be done." (Luke 22: 42)

56. *Two candles to light up the soul in darkness*

At the heart of her battles in following Christ, Maryam would use this effective weapon of obedience to win victory after victory. We know that among the Carmelites, obedience constitutes an essential part of the Rule; it is even one of the three vows that all religious pronounce. Maryam speaks to us, therefore, very forcefully about obedience as a pathway of light for the consecrated life. She states:

"One has to always obey, submit his will to that of his superiors. One must not make remarks. God does not like a soul who doesn't obey, who doesn't submit his own judgment. You must not bargain with Jesus. If you do anything for Him, do it completely. He doesn't like halves. A soul who does not give everything is a lukewarm soul, and Jesus vomits it from His mouth."

In a moment of ecstasy, Maryam told a Sister who was a little fearful:

"Practice only obedience to authority. Obedience and submission are two candles which light up the soul in darkness. It is in the dark times, in the terrible times, that one must allow himself to be guided by obedience."

Maryam received from Heaven another piece of advice. She said: "The Blessed Mother let it be known to me that obedience always preserves us from every misfortune and from all the snares of Satan."

Among the confessions of Satan, this one is worth mentioning:

"Six years ago, we began to attack a Carmelite Sister in Spain," said the demon. The first two years we did everything to inspire antipathy in her towards one of her companions; we pushed her not to talk to her, and not even to look at her: she did the opposite. The Master permitted that the two of them be placed by their superior in the same job; then, we tried in a special way to make her grow impatient; but she showed only the greatest support, the most perfect charity.

We tempted her against purity, against mortification, against humility, and always without success. We suggested that she see her superiors more often, especially the confessor; she went to them even less; we exalted her solid virtue, implying she didn't need frequent direction; she turned more often to the prioress and to the priest. When we prompted her to ask for extraordinary penances, she was content with those of the Rule. If we tried to convince her of her holiness, she confessed her pride in the presence of all the Sisters. That wretch always crushed us."

Satan made Maryam sometimes deaf, sometimes mute. But the person in authority had only to say, "In obedience, speak: in obedience, hear," and the novice spoke and heard.

57. *Levitation at the top of a lime tree*

So numerous were the mystic graces Maryam manifested that describing them all would require an entire book. But one among them touches particularly on obedience, and Maryam offers us here an enormous testimony on "holy obedience."

When she was in the Carmelite convent in Pau, the Sisters noticed her absence at supper one evening. They began to look for her, and a novice heard her singing in the garden: "Love! Love!" Looking upward, she noticed Maryam perched at the top of a lime tree, and she was swinging herself on a tiny branch which shouldn't have even held a bird. Alerted by the novice, the Prioress acknowledged the fact and became perplexed. What do you do in a case like that? She ended by calling to Maryam: "My Sister Maryam of Jesus Crucified, if Jesus wills it, come down, out of obedience, without falling or hurting yourself!" At the single word "obedience," still in her ecstasy, Maryam came down from the lime tree "her face radiant," while stopping gently on several branches to sing about love. "The minute she reached the ground", reported one of the Sisters, "as if to compensate our Mother and our Sisters for our anguish, she kissed us with a kind of anointing and with an affection impossible to express."

A number of times, people saw her climb to the top of trees on the ends of the branches. She would put her scapular in one hand and, grabbing the end of a tiny branch by its leaves with her other hand; would move nimbly in just the blink of an eye up to the top of the tree along its exterior. Once at the top, she swung herself on a small branch and sang the love of God, her face resplendent. Then she descended again like a bird from branch to branch, in all lightness and modesty. When she came down, she no longer remembered anything.

During her levitations on the high branches of trees, what was Maryam doing? According to her own accounts, she was conversing with the Lamb of God, because it was, He who called her to the top of the tree. These dialogues with her Celestial Spouse filled Maryam with happiness and light, as we can easily imagine. However, in a split second, she was ready to interrupt them the minute obedience required it of her. To interrupt a loving conversation with God in order to obey a prioress who had perhaps no compelling reason to demand that? We see there in Maryam the sign of a true life of union with God and of a mystically authentic life. The great majority of saints obeyed persons who did not reach one quarter of their spiritual level. Behind the person who exercises authority, the obedient one sees the hand of the Father, who directs events according to His divine wisdom. To obey authority is to obey God. If, on the other hand, you argue, convinced of your own human wisdom or logic, you only delay the accomplishment of the Father's designs.

One day, Jesus said to Maryam; "My daughter, obedience is to a soul what wings are to a bird."

58. One day, something clicks

The third weapon in this spiritual battle, to belong to the light, is charity. Maryam demonstrated all her life a profound charity towards those around her and certainly a great love for the Lord. I'd like to ask you this question: what is it that saved Maryam from sinking during those battles she had to take on? What sustained her was the immense love of souls that Jesus communicated to her.

The Savior, who went as far as death for each one of us, sees our souls clearly and the state of sin they are in. Maryam received this gift of seeing the offenses against God in souls, and she felt them deeply. She burned with desire to save these souls, in union with her spouse, Jesus the Savior. I have noticed that, for many saints, there came a particular day when something clicked inside them, and they reached a superior degree of charity.

The love of the Lord burns so fiercely in the holy soul that it welcomes torment, suffering and pain no longer as misfortunes that they must flee, but, on the contrary, as welcomed and blessed tools that can be used for the sake of redemption.

At that moment, when the click occurs, it is God who is taking the initiative. The sign of it is that, for the soul, the hardships become smooth. The suffering becomes a gentle joy. Not the suffering in itself — that would be masochism, and therefore, a perversion. As a matter of fact, suffering in itself is always an evil. But these people burn so much with the love of Jesus that everything that is part of God's work becomes a joy for them, precisely because of their loving union with Him. To follow Jesus in everything, on Mount Tabor as well as at Golgotha, that is their joy. Such is true love, pure love!

59. The heart of Christ beats in her chest

I believe that this union is the essence of the charity of Maryam! She lived within her soul the suffering of the passion of Christ, and she sustained in her heart His wounds; she endured His tortures in her body, and she lived all of that in thanksgiving! She loved Jesus so much! All of her crosses brought her into communion with the redemptive love of Christ.

So, we are not surprised to see that, given this source of love, it is the heart of Jesus Himself which beats in her chest. Attached to this source of love, she spent herself to the point of exhaustion in the service of her Sisters, in the service of souls.

Here are some of her words about charity, marvelous words of simplicity and profundity:

"Have a great deal of charity. Just as you prepare the way for your brother, the Lord will prepare for you. If you see stones along his path, remove them without his seeing it. If you see a hole, fill it without his seeing it. Make his path smooth. If you are thirsty and if someone gives you water, give this glass to your brother who is thirsty; although you may be thirstier than he, you are sure that the Lord will give you a drink from His hand." She also repeated to her Sisters without ceasing, "Love your Sisters more than yourselves!" When she was speaking under the inspiration of her Angel or that of the Holy Spirit (even a few saints who came to visit her), she would say to her superior, "Love the lambs which are entrusted to you; love them more than yourself!"

Maryam was visited supernaturally by certain saints, by certain angels, and by the Mother of God herself, who instructed her throughout her life. She was formed in her heart by the Blessed Mother and nourished by her wisdom.

60. The flowery native tongue

Having been born in Galilee to a poor family, Maryam had an unsophisticated language and always used very flowery phrases. She was a poet, even in her somewhat chaotic French! When she transmitted the teachings that came to her from on High, she presented them like little parables. She used imagery from everyday life.

That reminds us of the Bible and also of the language of another Galilean: Jesus of Nazareth!

Here are several stories which she liked to tell her Sisters:

"In order to enter Contemplative prayer, you must have weapons." So, a Sister asked her: "But what are these weapons for Contemplative prayer?" In response Maryam said:

61. "No prayer without a little hatchet!"

"When there are things which come to us, for example, distractions, thoughts outside of prayer, we have to arm ourselves with a little hatchet." So, the Sister said to her:

"But what is this little hatchet?"

"It's the hatchet of good will. Good will, that's the little hatchet which allows us to cut off at the root everything that sprouts and which is not of God, and which comes to bother us during prayer."

Regarding sin, Maryam recounts this magnificent parable, one to remember, because it is the cure for the tormented soul: "In Heaven, the most beautiful trees are those which had sinned most on earth. Why? Because they used their sins like manure, which they deposited at the foot of the tree." What a beautiful insight into God's mercy!

The teachings of Maryam overflow with hope! Maryam is not out to accuse or threaten the worst of sinners, but, on the contrary, wants to encourage his trust in Divine Mercy. Then the sinner understands that even his sin, can be changed by God into something positive in the service of the light. He puts his sin at the foot of the tree as one uses manure to fertilize the tree and help it bear beautiful fruit."

62. *Give hope to sinners!*

Even about pride Maryam speaks in a language of hope. "Those who are very proud by nature," she says, "are given a grace."

Why? She explains that because of it, they are obliged each day to discipline themselves against pride. They have to perform certain deeds to fight this evil tendency. Through this battle against pride, the Lord makes them grow precisely in humility. They will have to fight all their lives against their pride. But thanks to that combat, they will be glorified in humility in a very particular way. This is just another way of saying that each of the stubborn defects in our nature is a sign that the Lord wants to elevate us to a high degree in the opposite virtue! Magnificent! Only Jesus could find a way to use an evil to make us grow in goodness!

Maryam took as an example pride, but you could also say the same thing about egotism, impurity, or avarice. You see, Maryam transformed everything in the light of the Holy Spirit in order to encourage her Sisters, to give hope to sinners, to give joy back to broken hearts, to sustain those in pain.

63. *Oh, if only I was in good health!*

For people who were afflicted by disease, Maryam has words to restore peace. She observed in her Sisters certain thoughts which made them lose their peace when they were in the throes of illness. When one says, "Oh, if only I was in good health! I would do this thing for the Lord, I would do that good work for God, for my soul!" But Maryam shows us how those thoughts are pure illusions; because, in the very midst of illness, the Lord has us live out something important. If someone asks for a cure, let it be only for the Glory of God. "My God, if the cause of your glory demands it, if it is your will, if the good of my soul requires it. Please, heal me!"

Maryam was entirely oriented towards God and occupied with His glory. Nothing in her even resembled a focus on herself, quite the contrary! The Lord even permitted her to be unaware of the graces which passed through her. She saw herself as the least of the Sisters, the worst of sinners, and she considered it a great charity on the part of her Sisters that they welcomed her into the heart of the monastery.

64. The 'Ego' leads the world into oblivion

Maryam had no air of self-satisfaction about her. On this point she gave a lesson which is very striking in its clarity, and she had some succinct words to say about the "I." Regarding the "I," the infamous "Ego" which dies five minutes after we do, she said: "The Ego leads the world into oblivion. Those who have the 'I' carry sadness, anguish within them. You cannot have the 'I' and God together. If you have the 'I,' you don't have God, and if you have God, you don't have the 'I.' You don't have two hearts, you have only one. Everything succeeds for the one who has no ego. Everything makes him happy. Where there is the 'I,' there is no humility, gentleness, no virtue. You pray, you plead, and the prayer doesn't rise, doesn't reach God."

All of these reflections are words of wisdom.

65. The knowledge of hearts

Maryam was also blessed by the Lord with a gift that people call "the knowledge of hearts." How can we not think of the Curé of Ars or of Padre Pio? When they welcomed sinners into their confessionals, they saw in the depth of souls' certain sins which people didn't dare confess! "The knowledge of hearts" is a charism in the service of the mercy of God. In the course of her life, Maryam had the opportunity to practice on numerous occasions this charism in the service of her Sisters. As a matter of fact, she exercised it not only for her Sisters, but also for people close to the Carmelites. She even used it for the pope and certain prelates of the Church.

Let's cite several cases. A novice in her community was showing signs of spiritual uneasiness and anxiety; in short, she was not well, and no one was successful in finding the cause of her troubles. One day, the Lord said to Maryam, "Go see Sister so and so, and speak to her!" The Lord revealed then to Maryam that this Sister had a sin which had not been confessed, a serious sin from her past. Maryam went straight to the Sister and asked her:

"Have you truly confessed all the sins of your past?"

"Yes," answered the novice, in all sincerity. At least I didn't conceal any." Maryam said to her,

"And this particular sin, did you confess it?"

The novice experienced a shock and realized that she had been concealing this sin for many years. Quickly, she called a priest for confession and her peace was restored immediately. The Sister explained then to Maryam that she had repressed this sin even to the point of forgetting it. Now it was that sin which was the root of her profound spiritual uneasiness. On numerous occasions, Maryam was able to render service in this way to her own community.

66. Explosives under the Vatican? Visions and Prophesies

I am reminded of certain visions that Maryam received. She saw wars in the times to come and she asked her community to pray very hard. She also saw certain priests fall. She saw some of them seized by terrible temptations. She saw the descent of certain souls. In a very precise and concrete way, she saw, also, that in Rome, evil people were placing explosives under the Vatican to blow up certain parts of the buildings. So, with the permission of her superior, she managed to warn some of those concerned in Rome. Investigations revealed that she was right. A great misfortune was avoided. This particular deed attracted the attention of the pope himself, so much so that, later on, when she was delivering other messages from the Lord, she was very much listened to in Rome, as well as in the Carmelite Order. There had been proof that her inspirations truly came from the Lord.

Here I would like to point out the spirit which inspired the practice of this charism of knowledge in Maryam. She never wanted to know the future. She never intended to discover, through curiosity, the events to come or the mysteries of God. Certain lights were given to her without her asking for them. Besides, she did not accept it when people consulted her the way someone would consult a soothsayer, an astrologer, a fortune teller, a tarot card reader who claim to know the future. She was not an intermediary "sibyl" who would have uttered oracles as in the time of the ancient Greeks. Maryam's gift was, utterly and completely, an overflowing love in the service of the glory of God. If she sometimes delivered words of foreknowledge, it was to help souls. To help them do what? To help them be faithful and belong all the more to God. After having delivered the word she received, Maryam would withdraw herself entirely, like the prophets of the Bible. The prophet is someone who receives and transmits a word which comes from God. The message goes through the prophet and reaches the people. The prophet is only the messenger, the obedient servant of that message.

67. They suffer like fatherless orphans

That's very different from this modern mentality which consists in wanting to know everything about the future in order to be able to make plans accordingly, or just to satisfy curiosity. I believe this greediness for every bit of information comes from the fact that people don't believe they have a Father. Many of our contemporaries behave like orphans. They suffer like orphans! A child who has a father doesn't feel the need to know the plan of what's going to happen to him; he has confidence. The father, little by little, step by step, introduces his child to the things of life, to the realities that he will have to face. Maryam teaches us how to abandon ourselves to our Father in Heaven, who knows what we need, as Jesus tells us in Scripture. In this, Maryam is actually a forerunner of St. Thérèse of Lisieux, (France). The whole way of abandonment and of trust which Thérèse taught several years later, the "little way," as she would call it, was already prepared by this message of Maryam. (See footnote: Clarke, John. Story of a Soul: The Autobiography of St. Therese of Lisieux. Washington, D.C: ICS Publications, 1975).

68. Lebanon and Jerusalem

In addition, Maryam practiced this gift of prophesy for certain particular countries. Let's take the example of Lebanon. Maryam was very close to Lebanon because she had family roots there. She was a daughter of the Middle East, a pure-bred! The Lord showed her in advance the many and numerous sufferings which were waiting for Lebanon. I'd like to quote several passages, because it's remarkable to see today how these prophesies have been proven correct.

Maryam speaks first about Beirut. "Over Beirut," she says, "I also see something, a cloud which hovers over the city. It is red, green, and black." Note that at this time this flag didn't exist. Today, we know that it's the flag of Syria. She continued, "I smell blood, everywhere the odor of blood around me, as if there were a corpse." She goes on to say, "I see cisterns of blood." She adds, "In spite of all that, deep down I feel a joy which I cannot define."

In spite of all those revelations about Lebanon, over and above the tribulations and extreme distress which this country would have to endure, Maryam experienced a profound spiritual joy, which was a sign that a victory was being prepared for Lebanon and that the Lord was going to save this country.

Maryam speaks also of Jerusalem.

"I see over Jerusalem, in the air, a ball of fire. It seems to me that it is ready to fall. Prayer alone can stop it."

69. France, ask forgiveness, ask forgiveness!

Then Maryam speaks about France. Ever since her stay at the Carmelite convent of Pau and her trip to Marseille, the Lord had put into her heart an immense love for France. She compares France to a rose bush in the garden of the Lord. Jesus had spoken much about this rose bush to her. Maryam says that the rose bush is going to be trimmed by three pruning shears. There will remain only one branch, and it will be through this branch that God will do great things. She says that France has to be purified.

She says on behalf of the Lord: "France, ask forgiveness, ask forgiveness!" "France has done too much good in the missions, for God to abandon it. France will be holy, but it doesn't deserve it yet! If the people pray and convert, its trial will be small. If not, it will plunge lower and lower." Maryam says of the Lord: "He will do wonderful things in the heart of France." But Jesus told her that before it occurs, "a purifying filter must pass through, and France must be reduced to nothing, so that I may be at the head of the armies, so that all nations might say to one another: 'Truly, it is the Most High who is at the head of France!' Everyone will cry out as from one mouth, with one voice, in the same tone, even the impious ones."

To put it simply, in order to save France completely, God is waiting until it cries out to Him with all its heart. I believe that Maryam expressed through that message what other prophets have expressed: that France has a very privileged place in the plan of salvation for humanity.

Maryam was aware of that great mission, and she was very demanding of France. She wanted it to belong truly to God because, as the Lord said to her, "All that does not belong to God will be swept away." Of course, that is true for France just as it is for the rest of the world. We can find that in Scripture: "Every plant that my Father has not planted will be rooted up" Jesus tells us (Matt. 15: 13). France can begin

doing a serious examination of conscience before the coming
of the pruning shears!

70. A caress from God in the midst of her pots and pans

I give thanks to John Paul II for having raised up on the
altars this little humble peasant girl from Galilee, who comes
to remind us, with her childlike language, that mysteries are
revealed to the little ones. A soul which is totally abandoned
to God, knows God. From her first moment in this world,
Maryam had knowledge of supernatural realities; she understood intuitively the spiritual life. Maryam lived with God,
and her life was like a laying on of hands from Heaven to
Earth, a caress from God. All of this in the midst of her pots
and pans, of her tools, in the middle of the humblest, the
most hidden, even the most painful, work.

Maryam is truly the little child, who, in her natural poverty, welcomed the mysteries of God. She became for us a
witness of the invisible. She leapt forward a century to speak
to us, and I believe she landed in our century precisely because our century wants to separate itself from the mysteries
of God and to do without Him. Our society wants to explain
everything through science; it wants to explain man through
psychological mechanisms. It is fixed on the search for well-
being, which throws it into the agony of ill-being. Or worse
yet, it wants to plunge man into dubious spiritualities, like
those of the New Age, which denies the incarnation of God

as a basic principle. So, Maryam arrives like a bomb, a most pleasant bomb, to talk to us about things from on high and to remind us of our final destination.

Maryam lived with the angels. She lived with the Blessed Mother, and she allowed herself to be instructed from on high. On numerous occasions, when I've had the opportunity to speak about her to religious communities as well as to the young, to adolescents, I was always struck by one thing: Maryam goes straight to the heart!

71. *She opens the windows of our prisons*

Her words are very simple; that is why they reach deep into the hearts of people (all the translators of this booklet have fallen in love with her!). I remember certain adolescents in front of whom I would say to myself, "It's too bad I will have to go quickly through the mystical graces of Maryam. It's a language that they can't understand; they are not going to get it, and they're going to blow it off!" But, on the contrary, to my great surprise, it's precisely that which triggers a thousand questions! These young people are victims of a real conspiracy of silence on the part of adults about these realities of our faith, in particular about the meaning of our lives on earth and its finality. As a matter of fact, they have an infinite thirst for learning the truth — the unvarnished truth —and they appreciate the fact that Maryam doesn't mince her words!

In the West, we no longer want to speak about God, about the things of God, about the Word of God, and still less about the spiritual combat which we must take on, lest we be defeated by the Evil One. We are afraid of the opinion of others. The Evil One has succeeded in strangling us with fear, the fear of not doing everything like everyone else, the fear of appearing different. Pure slavery! The young are thirsty, more than ever, to know these realities of the life of God, because they are being raised without that. They are cruelly deprived of that. They gradually wilt by a lack of spiritual perspective. As a result, they are dying. I give thanks to God for having revived Maryam, for having revealed her in our era after more than a century of silence. She opens the windows of our prisons. She breaks down our leaden doors.

In her clear little voice of child-prophet, it's as though she was telling us today, "But as for God, it's simple! He is there! Listen to His voice, you will not die! You will live!"

Maryam, we give our thanks to you! When we look at your life, we see that what you say is true. But know this: your work is not yet finished. From the highest Heaven, please, pray for us and come to help us, as you helped your Carmelite Sisters and the poor who knocked at the door of your heart! Nothing less!

Words and Counsels from Maryam, compiled by Father Estrate

Be very charitable. When one of your eyes sees evil, close it and open the other one! Change everything to good!

If you love your neighbor, then you know that you love Jesus. Do not look at your neighbor without seeing the Lord, or you will fall into a very deep hole.

I am in God and God is in me. I sense that all creatures, trees, flowers are God's and also mine. I have no more will; it is united to God, and all that is God's is mine... I would like a heart bigger than the universe.

Without Mary, we would be lost. The enemy makes holes everywhere. Mary takes care of us better than the best of mothers.

When Jesus looks at His elect, His gaze makes the heart melt. Oh, that gaze!

It is sweet to hear someone speak of Jesus, but sweeter to hear Jesus Himself. It is sweet to think of Jesus, but sweeter to possess him. It is sweet to listen to Jesus, but sweeter to do His will.

Be attentive to little things. Everything is big in the eyes of God.

Only love can satisfy the heart of man. The good man is content with love and a little bit of land; but the wicked man, even with all the pleasures, the honors, and the riches he piles up, is always hungry, is always thirsty, is never satisfied.

Take great care to keep tranquility of heart, because Satan fishes in troubled waters.

It is my desire that you keep inner peace. Don't pay any attention to fears or scruples. Do what you can, be humble about what you cannot do, and consume all the vain fears that I call follies with the fire of love. (Maryam affirms with certitude what she maintains in this message: "From the Infant of Bethlehem.")

The Lord doesn't like it when we take back a part of our offerings. Offer Him all and give Him all.

Be small; be and remain small, so that the mother keeps you under her wings, as the hen keeps her little ones and chases them away when they are grown. Be small, small... Jesus will keep you. See the hen and the little chicks: as long as they are small, she feeds them with her beak, she hides them under her wings; they lack nothing. Be small, the Lord will keep you, He will feed you

This morning I was troubled, because I did not feel God. It seemed as though my heart was made of iron. I was not able to think about God, and I invoked the Holy Spirit. I said; "It is you who makes us know Jesus. The apostles remained a long time with Him without understanding Him, but one droplet of you made them understand Him. You will make me understand Him also.

Come, my Consolation; come, my Joy; come my Peace, my Strength, my Light!"

God is hidden in the fruit like the seed in the apple. Open an apple and you will find the seed inside the apple. Open the apple and you will find five seeds in the middle. God is hidden in the same way in the heart of man. He is hidden there with the mysteries of His passion, symbolized by the five seeds. God has suffered and man must suffer, whether he wants to or not. If he suffers through love, in union with God, he will suffer less and gain merit. The five seeds that are at the center of his heart will germinate and produce abundant fruit. But if he rejects the trial, he will suffer even more, without gaining any merit.

To her Sisters in the Carmelite convent, during her ecstasies

If each of the lambs looks at herself as the least of all, the Blessed Mother will be with her. Follow the word of Jesus. Don't ever get discouraged. Satan will come, furious, to tempt you; don't ever listen to him. Listen always to the Shepherd. Never, never listen to Satan; he is jealous. When he comes, humble yourself. If Jesus permits him to tempt you, it is to help you grow.

May the lambs always obey the Shepherd, may they love one another always; may they always practice humility, charity. Satan is jealous of you; but don't ever get discouraged. Follow the Shepherd. Satan does not like charity. He will try to put one person against another. Embrace each other; he will leave.

Satan will tempt you; be stronger than Satan. Temptation is good for you. It is the water which washes and renders you clean for Jesus. The strongest temptation is like the warm water which cleans us best.

Reflect well on this: today on the Earth, tomorrow under the earth.

Let us run even more to God the more we are tested. Rejoice if people despise you, because you are under the mantle of the Lord. If you are esteemed or honored, cry tears of blood, because the enemy will come to rob you. Robbers don't steal from the houses of the poor but from the houses of the rich.

I ask Heaven, Earth, the sea, the trees, all creatures: "Where is Jesus?" And all answer me in one voice: "In a righteous and humbled heart!"

Little sheep, love the one who slaps you and not the one who gives you kisses. If you defend yourself when someone slaps you, you will lose everything; but if you kiss the one who strikes you, God will keep you.

Satan is jealous; he tries by every means to make you lose your faith, to make souls fall: don't be afraid. Even when you don't feel the faith, you must live in humility and confidence. When we don't feel faith and yet keep moving forward in spite of our groanings and our tears, we endure a very meritorious martyrdom, provided that our lives are always turned toward Jesus.

Jesus has chosen you: be grateful to Him. Observe the rule well. If a novice doesn't observe the Rule, even if she performs miracles, send her away.

Never look at either the mistakes or the shortcomings of the Sisters. Keep to yourself the most difficult, the most painful things, in order to comfort the others. Think always good of others: excuse them. If you see a Sister spilling oil, think that she is lost in God, then pick up a rag to clean up the spill.

To the prioress: "Be without fear. When a Sister comes to tell you: 'My Mother, during prayer time I saw Our Lady, I saw Jesus, they told me such and such a thing,' respond to this Sister: "My daughter, take advantage of what you have seen and heard. This grace must bear fruit. By the fruits you will distinguish if this is a reality or an illusion." If the Sister remains content after you have spoken to her in this way, say to yourself: It is really Jesus, certainly. But if she goes away sad, say: it is Satan.

To a priest that was criticized: "Let them talk, let them say all they want. God is God! Even if all of Heaven and Earth turned upside down in order to shake a soul God looks at, they will be able to do nothing."

Little lambs, Satan will transform himself into an angel of light. With a little attention, you will always recognize him, because he will try, through his praises, to stir up the pride in you. Humble yourself, say: "I am but nothing, I am not worthy of any grace," and he will go away.

The Lord does not reproach you for having sinned, but for not having humbled yourself.

To love is not sufficient. To love and to work, that is everything. To love is to plant the seed; to work is to germinate, grow, and bear the fruit.

People asked her what they had to do to possess love. She stooped down, picked up a granule of dust, and, extending it to her questioner, she said: "You have to become as small as that."

The Autopsy on the
Body of Maryam

"Several hours after her death, a certain man named Carpani, who was a practicing physician, came to remove the heart. After the heart was taken out, it was put on a tray so that everyone could examine it. I was present with Don Belloni, Don Emilio, Don Teofilo, Don Giovanni Marta, and Don Ricardo Branca. We were all able to confirm that the heart bore the scar of a wound that would have been produced by a large metal blade. All the priests present and the nuns themselves were able to acknowledge this marvelous fact.

"We were able to confirm, also, that on the feet and on the hands, the Sister bore the scars of wounds similar to holes. On that subject, Don Belloni, confessor to Sister Maryam of Jesus Crucified, assured me that, during her lifetime, whenever someone held one of her hands up to the light, the flesh appeared transparent at the site of the stigmata.

"We were also able to confirm the visible outline of a large wound on the neck. Sister Cyprienne told me that Sister Maryam of Jesus Crucified, while in Alexandria, had been struck on the neck by a sharp weapon of a scoundrel who threw her into a ditch where she would have died, if the Blessed Mother had not saved her from this danger."

(Testimony of Monsignor Valerga, nephew of the Patriarch of Jerusalem)

Brief Resumé of Maryam's Life

1846	January 5, birth in Ibillin, Palestine.
	January 15, Baptism and Confirmation
1849	She loses her father and mother
1854	Adopted by her uncle in Alexandria, Egypt.
	First Confession and Communion.
1858	She refuses to get married.
1859/60	She works as a servant in Alexandria, Jerusalem and Beirut.
1863	Servant in the Najiar family in Marseille 1865. She enters the Sisters of Saint Joseph of the Apparition in Marseille, France.
1867	She enters the Carmelites in Pau and receives the habit on July 27.
1868	May 24, she experiences the transverberation of the heart.
	July 26 to September 4, a 40-day diabolic trial. Sept. 5-8, she is taken over by a heavenly spirit.
1870	August 21, she leaves for the Indies.

She arrives in Mangalore in November.

1871	Nov. 21, she pronounces her perpetual vows as a converse Sister.

1872   She returns to the Carmelite convent in Pau.

1875   August 20, she leaves for Palestine.

1876   The first stone for the convent in Bethlehem is laid.

1878   April/May, Trip to Emmaus, Mount Carmel, Ibillin, Nazareth, Mount Tabor and Bethlehem.

August 22, she falls and breaks her arm, the beginning of gangrene.

August 26, she dies at daybreak.

1983   November 13, she is beatified by John Paul II in Rome.

Her feast day is celebrated on August 26th.

Bibliography

The most basic book on Maryam's life and message is that of her spiritual director, Fr. Pierre Estrate, in French. It has not yet been translated into English. Most of our information and quotations have been taken from this source:

Brunot, Amédée. *Mariam, the little Arab: Sister Mary of Jesus Crucified* (1846-1878). Eugene, Oregon. Published by Carmel of Maria Regina, 1984. Print.

Buzy, Denis, scj, *Life of the servant of God, Sister Mary of Jesus Crucified: Carmelite lay-Sister who died in the odour of sanctity in the Bethlehem convent* (1846-1878) London: Sands, 1926. Print.

Buzy D. scj, *Thoughts of Sister Mary of Jesus Crucified,* ocd.

Estrate, Pierre. *Mariam, sainte palestinienne ou la vie de Marie de Jesus crucifie.* Nouv. éd. ed. Paris: P. Téqui, 1999. Print.

Foundress of the Carmel of Bethlehem. Jerusalem 1975. New Edition Jerusalem 1997

Her letters have been published in French at Les Editions du Carmel, 2011

See the link:

http: //www.carmelholyland.org/english/insmariam.htm

Sr. Emmanuel released 2 CDs where she tells Maryam's story from the book.

CD1: Maryam, the Little Arab

CD2: Maryam, the Little Prophet

Distribution in the English speaking countries, see website www.chidrenofmedjugorje.com

Illustrations

Maryam of Bethlehem

1. *Maryam's cell in Bethlehem.*
2. *Carmel of Bethlehem*

1. Maryam while in Bethlehem.
2. Chapel at the Carmel of Bethlehem

Jésus est Mon Amour et
Ma Joie, et sa croix est
Mon Plaisir et Ma Paix.
Mon cœur brûle nuit et
Jour de posséder le
Dieu d'Amour.
ô Machère Sr Agnès
Sr Marie de Jesus
crucifié.

Letter from Maryam to Sr. Agnes

1. Shepherd's field where the Angels appeared.
2. Place of the Nativity of Jesus

1. The door is very low to prohibit horses of the time from entering. Today,
we need to humbly bow the head before entering.
2. Entrance of the Basilica of Bethlehem, Basilica of the Nativity
at Bethlehem

Men studying Torah in Jerusalem

Children of Galilee

Olive harvesting in Bethlehem

Olive harvesting in Bethlehem

1. Lake of Galilee seen from the Mount of the Beatitudes.
2. Oriental Spices

Other Books from the Author

The Forgotten Power of Fasting
HEALING, LIBERATION, JOY …

"I read your book from cover to cover. Your words completely captivated me and have convinced me on the importance of fasting. I knew already the benefits of fasting, but I wasn't aware of all its attributes, that you explain so well. Reading this book one discovers fasting.

As we know, Our Lady in Medjugorje continuously insists on the importance of fasting, but we avoid putting into practice something when it means we have to make a sacrifice. We struggle to convince ourselves to actually fast.

The arguments you present, and the examples that you give in this book, show very clearly the reason why Our Lady insists so persistently on something so precious for the soul and the body, for the apostolate on earth and for the souls in Purgatory. I thank you for emphasizing such an important topic, very often mentioned in Sacred Scripture, so precious for the living and for the intercession of the dead.

The final part of your work, with the words from the saints, will convince even the most reluctant.

This book will be nothing less than a true discovery of fasting to whoever reads it."

Don Gabriele Amorth

Euro 7.00
Sister Emmanuel
© 1995 Children of Medjugorje
www.sremmanuel.org

Children, Help My Heart To Triumph!

At the height of the Bosnian War, Sister Emmanuel remained in Medjugorje with a few members of her community. During that time, memories of her father, a Prisoner of War during WWII, continually surfaced. Remembering how much he suffered, she felt a need to do something to spiritually help those on the front lines. Sister Emmanuel describes a call that she received at that time to appeal to the children for their sacrifices in order to alleviate the war. *Children, Help My Heart To Triumph* was written in response to that call. It describes for children how to make a 9-day novena of little sacrifices. Included is a coloring book that they can color and mail to Medjugorje where they will be presented at one of Our Lady's apparitions.

US $ 11.99
Sister Emmanuel
© 1996 Children of Medjugorje
Reprinted 2012 Includes Coloring Book
www.sremmanuel.org

The Amazing Secret of the Souls in Purgatory

It is not often that a book touches the soul so deeply. *The Amazing Secret of the Souls in Purgatory* is such a book. Maria Simma, deceased in March of 2003, lived a humble life in the mountains of Austria. When she was twenty-five, Maria was graced with a very special charism—the charism of being visited by the many souls in Purgatory—and being able to communicate with them! Maria shares, in her own words, some amazing secrets about the souls in Purgatory. She answers questions such as: What is Purgatory? How do souls get there? Who decides if a soul goes to Purgatory? How can we help get souls released from Purgatory?

US $ 8.99
© 1997 Queenship Publishing
www.queenship.org
www.sremmanuel.org

The Hidden Child of Medjugorje

"Reading "Medjugorje, the 90s" had left me dazzled and so deeply touched that it had literally pulled me to Medjugorje. I just had to see with my own eyes the spiritual wonders retold in that book. Now with "The Hidden Child," the ember of love for Mary has received a new breath of air—a Pentecostal wind. Sr. Emmanuel is indeed one of Mary's best voices! Congratulations for this jewel of a testimonial! I wouldn't be surprised if the Gospa herself turned out to be Sister's most avid reader."

Msgr. Denis Croteau, OMI

"Books are like seashells; at first they all look alike. However, they are far from being identical and their value varies greatly. Some of them are packed with riches and so well written, that they hide rare pearls within. Sister Emmanuel's book is one of those; it contains the most beautiful pearls, and with them enriches the reader. Through her accounts and anecdotes, the reader is pleased to meet people of great worth and to be filled with the teachings of so many events. Through this book, one will explore more fully a way still too little known: the way of the Queen of Peace."

Fr. Jozo Zovko, OFM

US $ 15.99
Sister Emmanuel
© 2010 Children of Medjugorje, Inc.
www.sremmanuel.org

Maryam of Bethlehem, the Little Arab

Who is this little Arab? Maryam Baouardy is a daughter of Galilee. Her life? A succession of supernatural manifestations worthy of Catherine of Sienna. Maryam shares the keys of holiness, including ways to defeat Satan himself. This is a book you don't want to miss?

US $ 5.00
Sister Emmanuel
© 2012 Children of Medjugorje, Inc.
www.sremmanuel.org
Available in E-Book

The Beautiful Story of Medjugorje
As Told to Children from 7 to 97

In this book, you will follow the experiences of six little shepherds, their shock when they saw the "Lady" appearing to them in 1981. You will see how Vicka and Jokov actually experienced the reality of life beyond this world, when Our Lady took them with her on the most extraordinary journey to Heaven, Purgatory and Hell.

You will learn how brave they were under persecution. You will be excited to know the mes—sages they share from a Mother who thinks only of helping us, who loves each one of us so much— including you in a very special way!

You will read about the powerful healings of bodies and souls happening there, as in Lourdes.

This is an adventure story, except that this story is true and is happening right now for you!

US $ 5.00
Sister Emmanuel
© 2012 Children of Medjugorje
www.sremmanuel.org
Available in E-Book

Peace will have the last word

The mercy of God is scandalous, it even borders on the extreme! In her engaging and lively style, Sister Emmanuel recounts real life stories and testimonies that take the reader's heart on a journey of God's mercy, passing through the prisons of New York, and into the confessionals of the Saints!

In these pages, a mosaic of photos and parables, the reader encounters the very depths of the human heart and is transported into the midst of scenes and situations that are as captivating as they are diverse. Through them we witness that much-desired peace that comes from Above, gaining victory over emptiness, futility and fear.

Here are words that many no longer dare to speak, and yet, they have the power to help rebuild a degenerating society. This book is a shot in the arm, an injection of hope that will hasten the time when, in the hearts of all, peace will have the last word!

US $ 13.99
Sister Emmanuel
© 2015 Children of Medjugorje
www.sremmanuel.org

Scandalous Mercy
WHEN GOD GOES BEYOND THE BOUNDARIES

Why Scandalous Mercy?

In these pages the reader will discover unexplored aspects of the Heart of God that you might think are crazy! Crazy with love! You will meet Mother Teresa, Maryam of Bethlehem, a Nazi criminal, a priest condemned to hell, a high ranking abortionist, a drug dealer from Brazil, a furious mother-in-law, a sick child...and in the middle of all this, the most beautiful Heart of Christ, who is calling ALL His children.

This beautiful selection of testimonies and "little flowers" picked from everyday life will capture the reader on two levels: first, the reader of this book will find his achy heart soothed and enriched by new ways to find hope in our difficult world today; second, he will be shocked to learn that these stories are true. They will make you laugh, cry, even tremble, but one thing is certain, they will all amaze you!

US $ 13.00
Sister Emmanuel
© 2015 Children of Medjugorje
www.sremmanuel.org

Medjugorje, Triumph of the Heart
REVISED EDITION OF MEDJUGORJE OF THE 90S

Sister Emmanuel offers a pure echo of Medjugorje, the eventful village where the Mother of God has been appearing since 1981. She shares at length some of the personal stories of the villagers, the visionaries, and the pilgrims who flock there by the thousands, receiving great healings. Eight years of awe have inspired this book. these 89 stories offer a glimpse into the miracles of Mary's motherly love.

US $ 12.95
Sister Emmanuel
© 2015 Children of Medjugorje
www.sremmanuel.org

Made in the USA
Monee, IL
27 March 2024

55919136R00075